25th Annual Conference of the European Association for Machine Translation (EAMT 2024)

Volume 2: Products & Projects

Sheffield, United Kingdom
24 – 27 June 2024

Editors:

Carolina Scarton
Charlotte Prescott
Chris Bayliss
Chris Oakley
Joanna Wright
Stuart Wrigley
Xingyi Song
Edward Gow-Smith
Mikel Forcada
Helena Moniz

ISBN: 979-8-3313-0477-5

Printed from e-media with permission by:

Curran Associates, Inc.
57 Morehouse Lane
Red Hook, NY 12571

Some format issues inherent in the e-media version may also appear in this print version.

Association for Computational Linguistics
209 N. Eighth Street
Stroudsburg, Pennsylvania 18360

Phone: 1-570-476-8006
Fax: 1-570-476-0860

acl@aclweb.org

Additional copies of this publication are available from:

Curran Associates, Inc.
57 Morehouse Lane
Red Hook, NY 12571 USA
Phone: 845-758-0400
Fax: 845-758-2633
Email: curran@proceedings.com
Web: www.proceedings.com

EUROPEAN
ASSOCIATION
FOR MACHINE
TRANSLATION

Proceedings of the 25th Annual Conference of the European Association for Machine Translation

Volume 2: Products & Projects

June 24-27, 2024
Sheffield, United Kingdom

Edited by:
Carolina Scarton, Charlotte Prescott, Chris Bayliss, Chris Oakley, Joanna Wright, Stuart Wrigley, Xingyi Song, Edward Gow-Smith, Mikel Forcada, Helena Moniz

Organised by

University of Sheffield

ZOO

Foreword from the General Chair

As president of the European Association for Machine Translation (EAMT) and General Chair of the 25th Annual Conference of the EAMT, it is with great pleasure that I write these opening words to the Proceedings of EAMT 2024, a special year since we are celebrating our 25th anniversary!

According to tradition, my first note of deep appreciation and gratitude goes to Celia Rico, Luc Meertens, Lucia Specia, and Maja Popović, Executive Board Members, who have moved to new adventures in their lives, after outstanding, and dedicated service to the EAMT community.

We have several milestones to celebrate this year, built upon the hard work of our Executive Committee (EC) and our community: upgraded grants for low-income and war zones and for Translation Studies, a record submission rate for research projects, continuous excelling submissions for the best thesis award, and one of the highest number of papers ever submitted to our conference (80 papers accepted)! I could not be prouder of our EC and the dynamics of our community.

The EAMT Executive Committee (EC) has been very busy. Luc Meertens (treasurer), Carolina Scarton (secretary) and Sara Szoc (preparing to become our secretary and supporting everything we do) have been tirelessly supporting all initiatives. André Martins and Celia Rico, our co-chairs for low-income areas, war zones and Translation Studies grants, selected 11 grantees, 6 applicants from Translation Studies and 5 from war zones (3 hybrid light and 8 in-person). Maja Popovič and Sara Szoc, our co-chairs for the Research Projects, selected 4 projects (equally distributed by students and general research projects calls) with a diverse set of topics. To all our co-chairs, my gratitude! The selection work is never an easy task and this year was particularly hard.

The same applied to the best thesis award – Barry Haddow, chair of the Best Thesis Award, had a very difficult time selecting a candidate, since the submissions were of very high quality. Our congratulations to Marco Gaido's thesis "Direct Speech Translation Toward High-Quality, Inclusive, and Augmented Systems"(FBK, Italy), supervised by Marco Turchi and Matteo Negri. Our congratulations extended to the two highly commended theses of Jannis Vamvas: "Model-based Evaluation of Multilinguality" (University of Zurich, Switzerland), supervised by Rico Sennrich and Lena A. Jäger; and Javier Iranzo-Sánchez: "Streaming Neural Speech Translation" (UPV, Spain), supervised by Jorge Civera and Alfons Juan.

EAMT, as full sponsor of the MT Marathon, would also like to highlight the outstanding work that the MT Marathon organisers conducted, enriching the vitality of our community with their projects and keynotes. A special thank you to the organising committee Lisa Yankovskaya, Agnes Luhtaru, Lisa Korotkova, Mark Fišel, Ondrej Bojar, and Barry Haddow for all the efforts on yet another successful MT Marathon event. Thank you, University of Tartu, for hosting the event.

Sheffield, United Kingdom! EAMT 2024 celebrates our 25th anniversary! Our conference will have a three-day, four-track programme put together by our chairs: Rachel Bawden and Víctor Sánchez-Cartagena (research: technical track co-chairs); Ekaterina Lapshinova-Koltunski and Patrick Cadwell (research: translators & users track co-chairs); Chatzitheodorou Konstantinos and Vera Cabarrão (implementations & case studies track co-chairs); and Mikel Forcada and Helena Moniz (products & projects track chairs). And backing up all the scientific components of our conference and filters of quality for the final selection: our reviewers. Thank you for your work and the alignment between all the chairs!

Continuing the successful event from Tampere, this year EAMT 2024 will also have an extra day for workshops and tutorials, organised by our co-chairs Diptesh Kanojia and Mary Nurminen. Once more, the submissions for workshops and tutorials largely exceeded our expectations for our second edition!

The programme will continue the tradition of including two keynote speakers, Alexandra Birch (Reader in Natural Language Processing in the Institute for Language, Cognition and Computation, School of Informatics, University of Edinburgh) and Valter Mavrič (Director-General of the Translation Service – DG TRAD – at the European Parliament). Our outstanding keynote speakers will demonstrate their extensive and global impactful work in translation studies and translation technologies.

EAMT 2024 would never be possible without the synergetic, sharp, enthusiastic, and hard working local organising team! What a dream and fun team to work with! Our local co-chair, Carolina Scarton (University of Sheffield, UK), who always supports the EAMT community and is always eager to do the best EAMT ever! Our local co-chair from ZOO Digital, Chris Oakley, also Charlotte Prescott (ZOO Digital, UK), Chris Bayliss (ZOO Digital, UK), Joanna Wright (University of Sheffield, UK), and Xingyi Song (University of Sheffield, UK). From the local organising support team, our thank you to Freddy Heppell (University of Sheffield, UK) and Tom Pickard (University of Sheffield, UK). Our special gratitude to the University of Sheffield and ZOO Digital for the joint efforts. You will surely make our 25th anniversary memorable!

The Sheffield team is working towards a special 25th anniversary. Carolina Scarton has been doing intensive work on organising and finding a home for the John Hutchins Machine Translation Archive. Carolina is deeply committed to respect John's wishes of making his library available to the community, and the former president, Mikel Forcada, and current one are fully supporting Carolina's initiatives. As an anticipation of such effort, the Sheffield team is working on presenting a sample of John's books for EAMT 2024 participants! Thank you, Carolina Scarton, for all the hard work on this. Within this topic still, a special thank you to Mike Hutchins, John's son, who is fully committed to make it happen and respect his father's vision of giving back to the community.

EAMT has been supported by generous sponsors in its initiatives along the years. This year is no exception. Our gratitude to our Silver sponsors: RWS Language Weaver, Translated, and Unbabel. To our Bronze sponsors: CrossLang, Pangeanic, STAR, and TransPerfect. Also to Apertium, our long standing collaborator sponsor, Springer, our Supporter sponsor for the Best Paper award, and our Media sponsors, MultiLingual. Your support is vital in our efforts to give back to our community through grants and other initiatives.

A note still to all our EAMT members and our participants! Without you no effort would make sense! Let us take this opportunity to create scientific collaboration and give constructive feedback. To fully enjoy the conference, please check our Code of Conduct at `https://eamt2024.sheffield.ac.uk/code-of-conduct`. I'm looking forward to seeing you all and celebrating our 25th anniversary with you!

It is our organisation's greatest wish to continue giving back to our community and to drive and be driven by our community's energy and enthusiasm. Reach out to us if you have new ideas or suggestions you would like to implement. We will try hard to accomplish it with you. Learn more about us at `https://eamt.org/`.

Helena Moniz

President of the EAMT
General Chair of EAMT 2024
University of Lisbon / INESC-ID, Portugal

Message from the Organising Committee

Ey Up!

We are delighted to welcome you to EAMT 2024 at Sheffield and celebrate its 25th anniversary. Sheffield, renowned for its rich industrial heritage and pivotal role in the steel industry, provides an ideal venue for "forging" collaboration and exchanging ideas. The outdoor cityprovides an ideal and welcoming environment for a thriving international community with a large number of students. The UK's greenest cityhas the Peak District National Park at its doorstep, being a not to be missed place for the most adventurous (looking for sports like bouldering and mountain biking) as well as for just relaxing on a short walk enjoying the views and hospitality of the Peak District's small villages. It is not rare that students end up staying in Sheffield and calling this fabulous place home (which is the case of some of us on the organising committee).

The University of Sheffield has also been key in developing Machine Translation research, being an active member of EAMT and part of its history. Memorable former members of the Sheffield community include: the late John Hutchins (creator of the MT Archive and author of the 1992 book An introduction to machine translation) was a librarian in Sheffield from 1965 and 1971; the late Professor Yorick Wilks (author of the 2008 book Machine Translation: Its Scope and Limits) was an emeritus professor and a former Head of the Computer Science department; and Professor Lucia Specia (the pioneer in the area of MT Quality Estimation and author of the 2018 book Quality Estimation for Machine Translation) was professor at the Computer Science department and former PhD supervisor of two of the local organisers.

ZOO Digital is a global provider of cloud-based localisation and digital distribution services for the media and entertainment industry. ZOO Digital offers a range of services including subtitling, dubbing, media processing, and distribution. The company uses proprietary technology platforms to streamline and manage the localisation process, making it more efficient and cost-effective. ZOO is a long-term partner of the University of Sheffield, being committed to support research in speech and text translation. They are also one of the most active sponsors of our UKRI AI Centre for Doctoral Training (CDT) in Speech and Language Technologies and their Applications and had their first sponsored PhD student working on the area of MT graduating in 2023.

We are especially excited about our conference venues, which showcase some of Sheffield's most iconic sites. Our welcome reception will take place in the stunning Sheffield Winter Garden, one of the largest temperate glasshouses in the UK. This beautiful indoor garden is filled with exotic plants from around the world. The conference dinner will be hosted at the Kelham Island Museum, a celebrated institution that chronicles the city's industrial history and innovation in steel production. Attendees will have the unique opportunity to visit the impressive River Don Engine, a steam engine that highlights Sheffield's engineering and industrial heritage. We are also thrilled to announce that ZOO Digital has generously funded a special pre-conference social event at the National Videogame Museum. This interactive museum celebrates the history and culture of video games, offering a fun and engaging way for attendees to unwind and connect with each other. Finally, participants that opt to attend the Kelham Island Food tour will be taken on a culinary journey of the area, visiting a range of eating establishments and enjoying generous samples at each stop, and gaining insight into the interesting history of this famous Sheffield district.

We extend our deepest gratitude to our Silver Sponsors (Language Weaver, Translated, Unbabel), Bronze Sponsors (AppTek, CrossLang, Pangeanic, STAR Group, TransPerfect), Collaborator (Apertium), Supporter (Springer Nature), Media Sponsors (MultiLingual), track chairs (Helena Moniz, Rachel Bawden, Víctor M Sánchez-Cartagena, Patrick Cadwell, Ekaterina Lapshinova-Koltunski, Vera Cabarrão, Konstantinos Chatzitheodorou, Mikel Forcada, Mary Nurminen, Diptesh Kanojia, Barry Haddow), keynote speakers (Alexandra Birch, Valter Mavrič), the programme committee, and authors.

Our special very thanks goes to the volunteers (Freddy Heppell, Tom Pickard, Edward Gow-Smith, and Shenbin Qian), administrative and technical support (Natalie Hothersall, Kim Matthews-Hyde, and James Bishop), events management (Gavin Lambert), and our emergency organisation support committee (Xi Wang and Mark Stevenson) whose hard work and dedication have made this conference possible. We also thank the EAMT executive committee for all the support provided and trust in our work, in particular Helena Moniz (also our general chair) and Sara Szoc. Finally, we also thank the Department of Computer Science, in particular Professor Heidi Christensen (Head of the Computer Science department) and Professor Kalina Bontcheva (head of the Natural Language Processing research group), for their support of our conference.

We invite you to explore and enjoy the city of Sheffield. Whether you are discovering its historical landmarks, enjoying its green spaces, or immersing yourself in its rich cultural offerings, we hope you find inspiration both within and beyond the conference sessions.

Carolina Scarton
(University of Sheffield)
(EAMT Secretary)

Charlotte Prescott
(ZOO Digital)

Chris Bayliss
(ZOO Digital)

Chris Oakley
(ZOO Digital)

Joanna Wright
(University of Sheffield)

Stuart Wrigley
(University of Sheffield)

Xingyi Song
(University of Sheffield)

Preface by the Programme Chairs

On behalf of the programme chairs, a warm welcome to the 25th annual conference of the European Association for Machine Translation in Sheffield, UK. Following last year's restructuring of the research track into two tracks, this year's conference programme is divided into four tracks, two dedicated to research (one for technical papers for development of MT techniques and one focused on translators and users of MT), an implementations and case studies track and a projects and products track.

The **Technical Research track** invited submissions on significant results in any aspect of MT and related areas, including multilingual technologies. As in previous years, this track proved the most popular of the four tracks, receiving a total of 46 submissions from 26 different countries. With one desk rejection and four paper withdrawals, 20 papers were accepted from 18 different countries, resulting in an acceptance rate of 43%, which is consistent with previous years. Six of the accepted papers are to be presented orally and the remaining 14 will be presented as posters.

Following current practices in the field, papers focus on neural MT (NMT), with several works also studying large language models (LLMs) for translation. Accepted papers represented a wide range of topics relevant to current interests in the field: context-aware MT (Appicharla et al., 2024; Gete and Etchegoyhen, 2024); the application of techniques for low-resource languages and scenarios (Chen et al. 2024; Guttmann et al.; Simonsen and Einarsson, 2024; Song et al. 2024) including sign language translation (McGill et al., 2024); attention to specific domains (Ploeger et al., 2024; Roussis et al. 2024) and to the challenges faced when dealing with them, e.g. for the incorporating of terminologies (Hauhio and Friberg. 2024). A number of works study LLMs (Chen at al, 2024.; Mujadia et al. 2024; Simonsen and Einarsson, 2024), a trend that is likely to continue in years to come. As a sign of the progress being made in the quality of MT systems, the EAMT 2024 technical research track also features several papers dealing with topics related to the alignment of MT outputs with the expectations of human users (Moura Ramos et al., 2024), including on the topics of toxicity (García Gilabert et al., 2024), formality (Wisniewski et al., 2024) and gender-inclusiveness (Piergentilie et al., 2024).

We would like to give our thanks to all the authors who submitted to the track and to the 72 reviewers, who provided feedback and insightful comments for the submissions received. We are particularly grateful to the emergency reviewers who agreed to review papers at the last minute in order for decision notifications to be sent out on time.

Translators and Users Track

The focus of the Translators and Users track is to cover a wide range of topics related to the interaction between human translators and other users of machine translation. The second edition of this track attracted 21 papers, with 18 accepted out of them which comprises 85.71% of acceptance. Five of the accepted papers will be presented orally and 13 will be presented at a dedicated poster presentation session. The accepted papers address the interaction between machine translation and its users from various perspectives and cover various aspects of machine translation use, including both interlingual and intralingual translation, looking into challenges and potentials of large language models, as well as correlating human and machine translation. They provide novel examinations of long-standing areas of interest for translators and users in this space including translation quality, MT performance, tools and methods to assist translators, and users' perceptions and attitudes towards MT.

Sui He experiments with prompts applying ChatGPT for automatic translation. The author compares translation briefs and what s/he calls persona prompts (assignment of a role of an author or translator to the system).

Claudio Fantinuoli and Xiaoman Wang explore correlation between automatic quality evaluation metrics with human judgements for simultaneous interpreting.

Serge Gladkoff et al. investigate the application of the state-of-the-art LLMs for uncertainty estimation of MT output quality, which is required to determine the need for post-editing.

Paolo Canavese and Patrick Cadwell analyse translators' perspectives on the use of machine translation and its impact in a specific institutional setting, i.e. the Swiss Confederation.

Marta R. Costa-jussà et. al. presents a novel multimodal and multilingual pipeline to automatically identify and mitigate added toxicity at inference time, which does not require further model training.

Celia Soler Uguet et al. compare performance of various LLMs for automatic post-editing and MQM error annotation across four languages in a medical domain.

Lise Volkart and Pierrette Bouillon compare human translation and post-edited machine translation from a lexical and syntactic perspective in two language pairs: English-French ad German-French. Their aim is to find out if NMT systems produce lexically and syntactically poorer translations.

Gabriela Gonzalez-Saez et al. describe their work on visualisation tools to foster collaborations between translators and computational scientists.

Maria Kunilovskaya et al. explore if GPT-4 can reduce translationese (specific feature of translated texts) in human-translated texts on bidirectional German-English data from the Europarl corpus.

Rachel Bawden et al. evaluate the effectiveness of a post-editing pipeline for the translation of scientific abstract demonstrating that such pipelines can be effective for high-resource language pairs.

Vicent Briva-Iglesias and Sharon O'Brien present a user study on professional English-Spanish translators in the legal domain, which focuses on impact of negative or positive translators' pre-task perceptions of MT.

Miguel Rios et al. explore the impact of automatic speech synthesis in a post-editing machine translation environment in terms of quality, productivity, and cognitive effort.

Silvana Deilen et al. evaluate performance of intralingual machine translation systems in the area of health communication.

Michael Carl looks into a way of using machine learning to validate the empirical objectivity of a taxonomy for behavioral translation data.

João Lucas Cavalheiro Camargo et al. conduct a survey aimed at identifying and exploring the attitudes and recommendations of machine translation quality assessment educators.

Bettina Hiebl and Dagmar Gromann propose to use the Best-Worst scoring for a comparative translation quality assessment of one human and three machine translations in the English-German language pair.

Adaeze Ngozi Ohuoba et al. investigate methods to detect critical and harmful MT errors caused by non-compositional multi-word expressions and polysemy. For this, they design diagnostic tests that they apply on collections of medical texts.

Nora Aranberri explores evaluation of the Spanish-Basque translations. The author compares evaluations done by volunteers and translation professionals.

We would like to thank the 28 colleagues that kindly gave their time and effort to review the papers submitted to this track. Your reviews were perceptive, detailed, and, above all, constructive. We would also like to express our special gratitude to those reviewers who stepped in at the last minute to provide extra reviews at short notice. Your collegiality was a great support to us.

Implementations and case studies track

Entering the second year with the Implementations & Case Studies track, we are excited to share the acceptance of 9 papers. These papers cover a wide range of topics, showing the latest advancements, challenges, and creative ideas in MT. The goal for this track remains unchanged: to report experiences with MT in organizations of all types (both industry and academia) and to share views and observations based on day-to-day experiences working within the dynamic field of MT.

The journey begins with Oliver et al. who detail corpus creation and NMT model training for legal texts in low-resource languages, shedding light on the intricacies of bridging linguistic gaps in specialized domains.

Continuing on this path, Eschbach-Dymanus et al. delve into the realm of domain adaptation of MT for business IT texts, offering valuable insights into the translation capabilities of LLMs.

Bechara et al. present the creation and evaluation of a multilingual corpus of UN General Assembly debates, underscoring the importance of robust linguistic resources in advancing our understanding of multilingual communication.

Additionally, Korotkova and Fishel present groundbreaking research on Estonian-centric MT, emphasizing data availability and releasing a back-translation corpus of over 2 billion sentence pairs.

Moving forward, Silveira et al. examine the suitability of GPT-4 in generating subject-matter expertise assessment questions, illuminating new avenues for leveraging artificial intelligence in language assessment.

Continuing in this direction, Nunziatini et al.'s research explores the advantages and disadvantages of using LLMs to make raw MT output gender-inclusive.

Berger et al. work in prompting LLMs with human error markings represents a significant step towards self-correcting MT, offering promising avenues for enhancing translation quality in specialized domains.

Vasiļjevs et al. present findings from a comprehensive market study on advancing digital language equality in Europe. They provide critical insights into the current landscape of multilingual website translation and introduce innovative open-source solutions aimed at bridging linguistic divides.

Lastly, Vincent et al. present an insightful case study on contextual MT in professional subtitling. This work sheds light on the practical implications of incorporating extra-textual context into the MT pipeline, offering valuable lessons for industry practitioners.

Together, these papers paint a vivid picture of the ever-evolving landscape of MT Implementations & Case Studies, showcasing the ingenuity, resilience, and collaborative spirit of the MT community.

Products and Projects track

This year we received 31 submissions and 30 papers were accepted. The selection will provide a plethora of products and projects being developed by our community with a rich set of topics, ranging from EAMT sponsored projects, European projects, services and products from distinguished industry and research players of our community. It will surely be a very lively session with the usual poster boasters (one of our EAMT conferences' favourite moments) and poster sessions. We would like to thank the 25 reviewers, who were drafted quite late, for their quick response and their timeliness.

Rachel Bawden
(Inria, Paris, France)

Víctor M Sánchez-Cartagena
(University of Alacant, Spain)

Patrick Cadwell
(DCU, Ireland)

Ekaterina Lapshinova-Koltunski
(University of Hildesheim, Germany)

Vera Cabarrão
(Unbabel, Portugal)

Konstantinos Chatzitheodorou
(Strategic Agenda, UK)

Helena Moniz
(University of Lisbon (FLUL)
INESC-ID, Portugal)

Mikel Forcada
(Prompsit Language Engineering
Elx, Spain)

Mary Nurminen
(Tampere University, Finland)

Diptesh Kanojia
(University of Surrey, UK)

Barry Haddow
(University of Edinburgh, UK)

EAMT 2023 Best Thesis Award (Anthony C Clarke Award)

For the 2023 best theses award, we received a total of 9 submissions; all were MT-related thesis defended in 2023. We recruited 20 reviewers to examine and score the theses, considering how challenging the problem tackled in each thesis was, how relevant the results were for machine translation as a field, and what the strength of its impact in terms of scientific publications was. Two EAMT Executive Committee members also analysed all theses. It became very clear that 2023 was another very good year for PhD theses in machine translation.

All theses had merit, all candidates had strong CVs and, therefore, it was very difficult to select a winner.

A panel of two EAMT Executive Committee members (Barry Haddow and Helena Moniz) was assembled to process the reviews and select a winner that was later ratified by the EAMT executive committee.

We are pleased to announce that the **winner of the 2023 edition of the EAMT Best Thesis Award** is **Marco Gaido's' thesis "Direct Speech Translation Toward High-Quality, Inclusive, and Augmented Systems"** (FBK, Italy), supervised by Marco Turchi and Matteo Negri.

In addition, the committee judged that the following theses, were **"highly commended"**:
Jannis Vamvas: "Model-based Evaluation of Multilinguality" (University of Zurich, Switzerland), supervised by Rico Sennrich and Lena A. Jäger

Javier Iranzo-Sánchez: "Streaming Neural Speech Translation" (UPV, Spain), supervised by Jorge Civera and Alfons Juan

The awardee will receive a prize of €500, together with a suitably-inscribed certificate. In addition, Dr. Gaido will present a summary of their thesis at the 25th Annual Conference of the European Association for Machine Translation. In order to facilitate this, the EAMT will waive the winner's registration costs, and will make available a travel bursary of €200.

Barry Haddow, chair, EAMT BTA award 2023
University of Edinburgh, UK

Organising Committee

General Chair

Helena Moniz, Universidade de Lisboa / INESC-ID

Local Organising Committee

Carolina Scarton, University of Sheffield
Charlotte Prescott, ZOO Digital
Chris Bayliss, ZOO Digital
Chris Oakley, ZOO Digital
Joanna Wright, University of Sheffield
Xingyi Song, University of Sheffield

Local Organising Support Team

Edward GowSmith, University of Sheffield
Freddy Heppell, University of Sheffield
Tom Pickard, University of Sheffield
Shenbin Qian, University of Surrey

Implementations Case Studies Track Program Chairs

Vera Cabarrão, Unbabel
Konstantinos Chatzitheodorou, Strategic Agenda

Products and Projects Track Program Chairs

Helena Moniz, Universidade de Lisboa
Mikel Forcada, Prompsit Language Engineering

Research Translators Users Track Program Chairs

Patrick Cadwell, Dublin City University
Ekaterina Lapshinova-Koltunski, Universität Hildesheim

Technical Track Program Chairs

Rachel Bawden, Inria
Víctor M. Sánchez-Cartagena, Universidad de Alicante

Thesis Award Program Chairs

Barry Haddow, University of Edinburgh

Workshops and Tutorials Program Chairs

Diptesh Kanojia, University of Surrey
Mary Nurminen, Tampere University

Programme Committee

Implementations Case Studies Track

Eleftherios Avramidis, Fred Bane, Adam Bittlingmayer, Marianna Buchicchio, Laura Casanellas, Laura Casanellas, Konstantin Dranch, László János Laki, Mara Nunziatini, Raj Nath Patel, Spyridon Pilos, Heather Rossi, Konstantin Savenkov, Marina Sánchez Torrón, Anna Zaretskaya

Research Translators Users Track

Sergi Alvarez-Vidal, Nora Aranberri, Lynne Bowker, Vicent Briva-Iglesias, João Lucas Cavalheiro Camargo, Michael Carl, Dragoș Ciobanu, Oliver Czulo, Joke Daems, Christophe Declercq, Dr. Silvana Deilen, Félix Do Carmo, Aletta G. Dorst, Maria Fernandez-Parra, Federico Gaspari, Junyan Jiang, Ramunė Kasperė, Dorothy Kenny, Maarit Koponen, Rudy Loock, Lieve Macken, Antoni Oliver, David Orrego-Carmona, Maria Del Mar Sánchez Ramos, Celia Rico, Carlos S C Teixeira, Susana Valdez, Mihaela Vela, Lucas Nunes Vieira

Technical Track

Sweta Agrawal, Eleftherios Avramidis, Parnia Bahar, Loic Barrault, Magdalena Biesialska, Sheila Castilho, Chloé Clavel, Éric Villemonte De La Clergerie, Raj Dabre, Aswarth Abhilash Dara, Miguel Domingo, Hiroshi Echizenya, Cristina España-Bonet, Miquel Esplà-Gomis, Marcello Federico, Marco Gaido, Aarón Galiano-Jiménez, Mattia Antonino Di Gangi, Thanh-Le Ha, Rejwanul Haque, Rebecca Knowles, Philipp Koehn, Maria Kunilovskaya, Gregor Leusch, Andreas Maletti, Antonio Valerio Miceli Barone, Kenton Murray, Masaaki Nagata, Toshiaki Nakazawa, Jan Niehues, Constantin Orasan, Daniel Ortiz-Martínez, Pavel Pecina, Stephan Peitz, Sergio Penkale, Andrei Popescu-Belis, Maja Popovic, Juan Antonio Pérez-Ortiz, Tharindu Ranasinghe, Natalia Carolina Alencar De Resende, Miguel Rios, Rudolf Rosa, Fatiha Sadat, Benoît Sagot, Beatrice Savoldi, Yves Scherrer, Djamé Seddah, Rico Sennrich, Dimitar Shterionov, Michel Simard, Patrick Simianer, Mirella De Sisto, Felix Stahlberg, Katsuhito Sudoh, Felipe Sánchez-Martínez, Aleš Tamchyna, Joël Tang, Ayla Rigouts Terryn, Arda Tezcan, Jörg Tiedemann, Antonio Toral, Masao Utiyama, Vincent Vandeghinste, Dušan Variš, David Vilar, Martin Volk, Trang Vu, Taro Watanabe, Minghao Wu, François Yvon, Biao Zhang, Dakun Zhang

Thesis Award

Rachel Bawden, Daniel Beck, Alexandra Birch, Ondřej Bojar, Bill Byrne, Vera Cabarrão, Sheila Castilho, Anna Currey, José G. C. De Souza, Miquel Esplà-Gomis, Marcello Federico, Mikel L. Forcada, Liane Guillou, Diptesh Kanojia, Philipp Koehn, Mary Nurminen, Constantin Orasan, John E. Ortega, Santanu Pal, Danielle Saunders, Carolina Scarton, Xingyi Song, Felix Stahlberg, Antonio Toral, Marina Sánchez Torrón, Bram Vanroy, Marcely Zanon Boito

Keynote Talk

Harnessing the benefits of machine translation at the European Parliament: from current practices to future possibilities

Valter Mavrič
European Parliament
24-06-2024 11:00:00

Abstract: Machine translation (MT) is an essential tool for one of the largest institutional translation providers in the world: the European Parliament's Directorate-General for Translation (DG TRAD). DG TRAD is home to 24 language units that embody and put into practice one of the core democratic principles of the European Union: multilingualism. In this complex environment, MT has become an integral part of DG TRAD's work, helping it to manage an ever-growing volume of translation requests and allowing it to focus on the unique value that only humans can bring to the translation process.
The MT technology used in DG TRAD is a focal point of cooperation between the EU institutions and is constantly evolving. To best harness the benefits, DG TRAD relies on a dedicated team that carries out tests to explore the best ways of using MT for DG TRAD's content.
This presentation will tell you, from a user's perspective, about DG TRAD's journey to identify the most efficient ways of working with MT. Here are some of the questions we will cover:

- How well does MT handle the European Parliament's content? Do all languages produce the same results? How does MT quality vary based on the type of content?
- How does MT improve efficiency? What efforts are still necessary after integrating MT into DG TRAD's workflow?
- What about clear language? How well does MT perform in this area?

Finally, we will look at the new areas DG TRAD is exploring in this age of artificial intelligence (AI) and where we see that further research could provide added value.

Bio: Valter Mavrič is Director-General of the Translation Service (DG TRAD) at the European Parliament (since 2016), where he was previously acting Director-General (from 2014), Director (from 2010) and Head of the Slovenian Translation Unit (from 2004). With an MA in applied linguistics and further training in translation, interpretation, linguistics and management, he has a long experience as manager, translator, interpreter and teacher of languages. He works in Slovenian, Italian, English, French, and Croatian and is currently preparing a PhD in strategic communication.

Keynote Talk
Translation and LLMs

Alexandra Birch
School of Informatics, University of Edinburgh
26-06-2024 09:15:00

Abstract: What is the future of translation research in the era of large language models? Brown et al. in 2020 showed that prompting GPT3 with a few examples of translation could result in translations which were higher quality than SOTA supervised models at the time (into English and only for French, German). Until this point, research on machine translation had been central to the field of natural language processing, often attracting the most submissions in annual NLP conferences and leading to many breakthroughs in the field. Since then, there has been enormous interest in models which can perform a wide variety of tasks and interest in translation as a separate sub-field has somewhat diminished. However, translation remain a compelling and widely used technology. So what is the promise of LLMs for translation and how should we best use them? What opportunities do LLMs unlock and what challenges remain? How can the field of translation still contribute to NLP? I will touch on some of my own research but I focus on these broader questions.

Bio: Alexandra Birch is a Reader in Natural Language Processing in the Institute for Language, Cognition and Computation (ILCC), School of Informatics, University of Edinburgh. She is a leader of the StatMT group and a co-founder of Aveni.ai - an award winning startup in speech analytics and conversational AI. Her main research focuses on machine translation and multilingual dialogue, but she has a broad interest in leveraging NLP to create compelling applications that improve people's lives.

Tutorial
Linguistically Motivated Neural Machine Translation

Haiyue Song, Hour Kaina, Raj Dabre
National Institute of Information and Communications Technology (NICT), Japan
27-06-2024 09:00:00

Abstract: In this tutorial, we focus on a niche area of neural machine translation (NMT) that aims to incorporate linguistics into different stages in the NMT pipeline, from pre-processing to model training to evaluation. We first introduce the background of NMT and fundamental analysis tools, such as word segmenters, part-of-speech taggers, and dependency parsers. We then cover topics including 1) word/subword segmentation, and character decomposition during MT data pre-processing, 2) incorporating direct and indirect linguistic features into NMT models, and 3) fine-grained linguistic evaluation for MT systems. We reveal the impact of orthography, syntax, and semantics information on translation performance. This tutorial is mainly aimed at researchers interested in the intersection of linguistics and low-resource machine translation. We hope this tutorial inspires and encourages them to develop linguistically motivated high-quality MT systems and evaluation benchmarks.

Panel

LLMs and Machine Translation for Low-Resource Languages: Bridging Gaps or Widening Divides?

24-06-2024 15:00:00 - 16:00:00

LLMs such as ChatGPT, Claude and Gemini 1.5 have come to dominate the AI landscape, through their ability to perform well across a wide range of tasks and languages. They have excellent abilities in machine translation for high-resource languages, often performing on par with dedicated translation models, and with exciting use-cases including stylization, post-editing, and human-in-the-loop approaches. Nevertheless, these models' capabilities are much more limited in languages with less digital representation: performance in lower-resource languages can be regarded as a byproduct rather than a focus and the reliance on English language training data reinforces English language cultural hegemony, with particularly high representation of American English cultural knowledge in model weights. In downstream evaluation, claims of multilinguality typically belie the dependence on English-centric data: the FLORES dataset, for example, which contains MT evaluation data in over 200 languages, is largely translated from English. This panel will explore the challenges and opportunities associated with LLMs for translating low-resource languages, investigating the dangers of exacerbating existing linguistic and cultural biases, the potential of LLMs to democratise information access, and how to ensure that these models benefit rather than marginalise underrepresented linguistic communities.

Panelists:

Adaeze Ngozi Ohuoba, University of Leeds, UK Adaeze Ngozi Ohuoba is a PhD researcher at the School of Languages, Cultures and Societies, University of Leeds. Her PhD research focuses on using large language models to detect and predict English medical source texts that could produce potentially harmful outputs when machine translated into a low-resource language like Igbo. Prior to commencing her PhD studies, she worked as a lecturer at the Department of Foreign Language and Translation Studies, Abia State University, Nigeria. She is also a freelance translator/ editor specialising in legal, medical and literary translations from French/Igbo into English and English/French into Igbo. Her research interests include Machine Translation for Low-Resourced Languages, Computational Linguistics, French as a Foreign Language and Language in Health

Alexandra Birch, University of Edinburgh, UK Alexandra Birch is a Reader in Natural Language Processing in the Institute for Language, Cognition and Computation (ILCC), School of Informatics, University of Edinburgh. She is a leader of the StatMT group and a co-founder of Aveni.ai - an award winning startup in speech analytics and conversational AI. Her main research focuses on machine translation and multilingual dialogue, but she has a broad interest in leveraging NLP to create compelling applications that improve people's lives.

Chris Oakley, ZOO Digital, UK Chris Oakley is the Chief Technology Officer (CTO) of ZOO Digital, a leading provider of cloud-based localization and digital distribution services for the global entertainment industry. With a career spanning over two decades in the technology and digital media sectors, Chris brings a wealth of experience and a visionary approach to his role at ZOO Digital. As CTO, Chris Oakley is responsible for overseeing the development and implementation of cutting-edge AI and ML technologies that power ZOO Digital's innovative services. Under his leadership, the company has continued to pioneer advancements in AI and ML cloud-based solutions, enabling efficient and scalable workflows for the localization and distribution of movies, TV shows, and other digital content.

Helena Moniz, President of EAMT & IAMT. University of Lisbon, Portugal. INESC-ID, Portugal Helena Moniz is the President of the European Association for Machine Translation (2021-) and President of the International Association for Machine Translation (2023-). She is also the Vice-Coordinator of the Human Language Technologies Lab at INESC-ID, Lisbon. Helena is an Assistant Professor at the School of Arts and Humanities at the University of Lisbon, where she teaches Computational Linguistics, Computer Assisted Translation, and Machine Translation Systems and Post-editing. She is now in a very exciting project, coordinated by Unbabel, the Center for Responsible AI (https://centerforresponsible.ai), within the Portuguese Recovery and Resilience Plan, as Chair of the Ethics Committee. Helena graduated in Modern Languages and Literature at the School of Arts and Humanities, University of Lisbon (FLUL), in 1998. She took a Teacher Training graduation course in 2000, a Master's degree in Linguistics in 2007, and a PhD in Linguistics at FLUL in cooperation with the Technical University of Lisbon (IST) in 2013. She has been working at INESC-ID/CLUL since 2000, in several national and international projects involving multidisciplinary teams of linguists and speech processing engineers. Within these fruitful collaborations, she participated in more than 20 national and international projects. From 2015/09 to 2024/04, she was the PI of a bilateral project between INESC-ID and Unbabel, a translation company combining AI + post-editing, working on scalable Linguistic Quality Assurance processes for crowdsourcing. She was responsible for the implementation in 2015 of the MQM metric, the creation of the Linguistic Quality Assurance processes developed at Unbabel for Linguistic Annotation and Editors' Evaluation. She also worked on research projects, involving Linguistics, Translation, and Responsible AI, and products developed by the Labs Team, mostly cultural transcreation, high risk products, and silently controlled language metrics for dialogues. In a sentence, she is passionate about Language Technologies in a human-centric perspective and always feels like a child eager to learn!

Mirko Lorenz, Deutsche Welle, Germany Mirko Lorenz is an Innovation Manager working for Deutsche Welle, Germany's international broadcaster. He has been a member of the Research and Cooperation Team (ReCo) since 2008. One main outcome of his work is plain X, a 4-in-1 software to simplify content adaptation. In plain X, users can transcribe, translate, subtitle, and create (synthetic) voice-overs. Mirko has a master's in economics and history from the University of Cologne and a professional background in journalism. He co-founded Datawrapper, a tool to create charts and maps which is used in many large newsrooms worldwide.

Valter Mavrič, DG TRAD, European Parliament Valter Mavrič is Director-General of the Translation Service (DG TRAD) at the European Parliament (since 2016), where he was previously acting Director-General (from 2014), Director (from 2010) and Head of the Slovenian Translation Unit (from 2004). With an MA in applied linguistics and further training in translation, interpretation, linguistics and management, he has a long experience as manager, translator, interpreter and teacher of languages. He works in Slovenian, Italian, English, French, and Croatian and is currently preparing a PhD in strategic communication.

Moderator: Edward Gow-Smith, University of Sheffield, UK
Moderator: Carolina Scarton, University of Sheffield, UK

Table of Contents

Products & Projects

Transitude: Machine Translation on Social Media: MT as a potential tool for opinion (mis)formation

Khetam Al Sharou
SALIS/ADAPT Centre,
Dublin City University, Ireland
khetam.alsharou@dcu.ie

Joss Moorkens
SALIS/ADAPT Centre,
Dublin City University, Ireland
joss.moorkens@dcu.ie

Abstract

Misinformation on social media is a concern for content creators, consumers and regulators alike. Transitude looks at misinformation generated by machine translation (MT) through distortion of the intention and sentiment of text. It is the first study of MT's impact on the formation of users' views of society through refugees in Ireland. It extends current MT evaluation methods with a new quality evaluation framework, producing the first dataset annotated for information distortion. It provides insights into the risks of relying on MT, with recommendations for users, developers, and policymakers.

1 Previous Research

The spread of misinformation on social media has attracted collective efforts nationally and internationally. For example, the Irish government proposed the 2020 Online Safety and Media Regulation Bill to regulate online activities and tackle harmful content. However, such initiatives focus on source texts, overlooking machine translation (MT) use, which is embedded into social media platforms. MT as a translation tool carries risks in terms of misinformation as it can sometimes deliver misleading translation where the meaning becomes different from what was intended, leading to major consequences. For example, Facebook's MT once provided 'attack them' as a translation for 'good morning', prompting the Israeli police to arrest the Palestinian author of the message.[1] Highlighting the need to consider MT and its implications is vital for any multilingual/multicultural society. Recent humanitarian crises such as the Syrian refugee crisis emphasised the importance of communication and the consequences of misinformation. These populations rely on MT to stay informed (Marlowe, 2020). Commercial MT systems are not trained on conversational user-generated content (UGC), which is mostly written in colloquial, abbreviated language, using symbols and hashtags (Al Sharou et al., 2021). Previous research revealed that MT tends to generate critical errors when translating UGC (Al Sharou and Specia, 2022). Social media posts often contain political or social opinions, expressed with a specific purpose (Xiong and Fiu, 2014). Such content depends heavily on persuasive language to influence opinions, and employs irony, sarcasm and/or metaphor. However, there is no guarantee that MT preserves the intention and sentiment of the original. As a result, readers of the translation may form a different opinion to the one intended. Transitude's research objectives (RO) are: 1. Provide an account of MT's role in information sharing on social media. 2. Estimate MT's role in forming asylum seekers and refugees' views of, and attitudes towards, a new society. 3. Propose recommendations on how the risks of using MT can be mitigated.

2 Research Design and Methodology

Transitude employs analytical frameworks, drawing on Translation Studies models (text in context,

[1] https://www.theguardian.com/technology/2017/oct/24/facebook-palestine-israel-translates-good-morning-attack-them-arrest

Proceedings of the 25th Annual Conference of the European Association for Machine Translation (Volume 2), pages 2–3
June 24-27, 2024 ©2024 European Association for Machine Translation

focusing on intentionality and sentiment) (Hatim, 1997; Van Dijk, 1998) that are typically used to judge human translation, and Natural Language Processing techniques (keyword extraction and automatic sentiment analysis). Target participants are Arabic-speaking Syrian and Iraqi asylum seekers and refugees (AS&Rs) living in Ireland.

2.1 MT use on social media

A review of how MT is documented and used on social media was conducted and presented in Vieira and Al Sharou (forthcoming). Preliminarily content analysis of MT on the X platform was also carried out on a set of posts/tweets (4120), collected using the NewsWhip Spike platform. From this dataset, 500 tweets with a focus on MT were manually identified and categorised as Neutral, Positive or Negative. Around half of the tweets (221) showed that users are not satisfied with its quality with only 68 tweets revealing a positive perception of MT. MT is utilised for translating restaurant signs, news articles, menus, and songs and employed across various contexts including journalism, medical, and refugee assistance. Google Translate is the most commonly used, followed by DeepL and ChatGPT. Future work will include a survey to explore whether Arabic-speaking AS&Rs use MT on social media.

2.2 MT's role in forming AS&Rs' attitudes

RO2 will involve two stages of analysis:

- **Content-oriented quality assessment**: a source-target type of linguistic analysis will be used to identify linguistic changes in the message caused by the MT to show its role in forming AS&Rs' attitudes. Opinion-based posts with a focus on immigration, racism and discrimination, and political parties will be selected.
- **Survey 2**: The project will carry out a target-language quality assessment of MT's impact. Sets of opinion-based posts (30 posts in total) will be selected to examine the opinions formed by AS&Rs after reading the machine-translated version of the posts. Machine distortions that could have altered their interpretation will be examined.

2.3 MT risks and mitigations

To meet RO3, 30-minute interviews will be conducted to further understand AS&Rs' experience with MT and how it affects their integration into society. The interviews will address the topic from a socio-technical perspective and will consider policy options to address MT's impact on users and society. This in turn could influence Ireland's future policies to reduce online misinformation. Guidance for users to avoid misunderstandings due to MT will be based on MT literacy framework (Bowker and Buitrago Ciro, 2019).

Acknowledgment

Transitude is a two-year project (Dec 2023 – Nov 2025), funded by the Irish Research Council as part of the GOI Post-doctoral Fellowship scheme. It is led by Dr Khetam Al Sharou and mentored by Dr Joss Moorkens, School of Applied Language and Intercultural Studies (SALIS) at DCU, Ireland.

References

Al Sharou, Khetam, and Lucia Specia. 2022. A Taxonomy and Study of Critical Errors in Machine Translation. *Proceedings of the 23rd Annual Conference of the European Association for Machine Translation*, Ghent, Belgium, 171–180.

Al Sharou, Khetam, Zhenhao Li, and Lucia Specia. 2021. Towards Better Understanding of Noise in Natural Language Processing. *Proceedings of the International Conference on Recent Advances in Natural Language Processing*, online, 53–62.

Bowker, Lynne, and Jairo Buitrago Ciro. 2019. *Machine translation and global research: Towards improved machine translation literacy in the scholarly community*, Emerald Group Publishing.

Department of Tourism, Culture, Arts, Gaeltacht, Sport and Media. 2021. Online Safety and Media Regulation Bill, online: https://www.gov.ie/en/publication/d8e4c-online-safety-and-media-regulation-bill/.

Hatim, Basil. 1997. *English-Arabic/Arabic-English Translation: A Practical Guide*, London: Saqi Books.

Marlowe, Jay. 2020. Refugee resettlement, social media and the social organization of difference. *Global Networks*, 20(2), 274-291.

Van Dijk, Teun A. 1998. *Opinions and ideologies in the press*. In Bell, Allan, and Peter Donald Garrett. Approaches to media discourse. Wiley-Blackwell. 21–63.

Vieira, Lucas Nunes, and Khetam Al Sharou. forthcoming. Everyday machine translation: Across digital and physical environments, *Routledge Handbook of Translation Technology and Society*.

Xiong, Fei, and Yun Liu. 2014. Opinion formation on social media: an empirical approach. *Chaos: An Interdisciplinary Journal of Nonlinear Science*, 24(1): 130.

Lightweight Neural Translation Technologies for Low-Resource Languages

Felipe Sánchez-Martínez, Juan Antonio Pérez-Ortiz, Víctor M. Sánchez-Cartagena, Andrés Lou, Cristian García-Romero, Aarón Galiano-Jiménez, Miquel Esplà-Gomis

Dep. de Llenguatges i Sistemes Informàtics, Universitat d'Alacant
E-03690 Sant Vicent del Raspeig (Spain)

https://transducens.dlsi.ua.es/lilowla/
{fsanchez, japerez}@dlsi.ua.es

1 Project Overview

The LiLowLa[1] ("Lightweight neural translation technologies for low-resource languages") project, funded by the Spanish Government and the European Regional Development Fund, aims to enhance machine translation (MT) and translation memory (TM) technologies, particularly for low-resource language pairs,[2] where adequate linguistic resources are scarce.[3] Additionally, the project seeks to optimize web crawling methods to gather relevant data for low-resource languages effectively while avoiding unnecessary downloads, thereby reducing crawling times and enabling the acquisition of larger parallel corpora.

The scarcity of linguistic resources is often a result of the low commercial interest in the language pair in question, frequently stemming from the economic constraints of the speaking communities. This also implies that translation technologies developed for low-resource language pairs are likely to be utilized in environments with limited computing capabilities; for this reason, the project focuses on lightweight technologies.

2 Objectives

We define the following objectives:

1. The improvement of the efficiency, robustness and applicability of neural MT systems involving low-resource language pairs.

2. The improvement of web crawling methods to avoid downloading documents that end up being useless after their processing.

3. The widening of the applicability of TMs in professional computer-aided translation (CAT) tools by allowing them to exploit monolingual corpora when MT is not a viable option or when the database of existing translations is not sufficiently large.

To attain these objectives, the project focuses on investigating how to make neural MT significantly more robust and efficient by distilling the knowledge in large pre-trained neural models initially developed for high-resource language pairs, such as NLLB-200, and researching new lightweight data augmentation techniques to make the most of the scarce resources available. It also concentrates on the development of smart focus crawlers to improve current corpus crawling methods, and on the integration of cross-lingual sentence embeddings into CAT tools to permit the search of translation proposals in monolingual corpora.

3 Languages of interest

In addition to the improvement of translation technologies for low-resource language pairs, LiLowLa seeks to build corpora and translation models for a number of languages selected on the basis of social impact and the preservation of their cultural heritage:

- Pairs consisting of Spanish and another language of Spain, including Aragonese, Asturleonese, Aranese, Basque, Catalan and Galician.

- Pairs made of Spanish and Mayan languages spoken in Guatemala and Mexico, such as K'iche', Yucatec, Q'eqchi', Mam, Tzeltal and Kaqchikel.

[1] https://transducens.dlsi.ua.es/lilowla/

[2] The term *low-resource language pair* is commonly used to refer to a combination of two languages for which there are few bilingual resources.

[3] The project will run from September 2022 to August 2025.

Proceedings of the 25th Annual Conference of the European Association for Machine Translation (Volume 2), pages 4–5
June 24-27, 2024 ©2024 European Association for Machine Translation

4 Expected results

As a result of the execution of the project we plan to deliver:

1. A smart bilingual focus crawler guiding the crawling towards webpages more likely to contain parallel content; thus facilitating quicker discovery and reducing the time and bandwidth needed for acquiring parallel corpora.
2. A multi-task data augmentation method able to get the most of the available parallel corpora and that can be easily integrated in current training workflows.
3. A method for the generation of synthetic parallel sentences from large pre-trained models in the absence of training bilingual corpora, for the purpose of training small student models for low-resource language pairs.
4. A method overcoming the main limitation of TM software —the scarcity of in-domain translation memories— by allowing the retrieval of translation proposals from monolingual corpora, which are much more abundant.
5. Monolingual and bilingual corpora for the languages of interest to the project.
6. Standard test sets based on FLORES+ for targeted languages.
7. Translation models with a reduced size for the languages of interest to the project obtained by distilling the knowledge of large pre-trained models like NLLB-200.

5 Resources

Corpora and software developed as part of the project will be released under free/open-source licenses. In what follows we provide an incomplete list of software and corpora released so far:[4]

MATiLDA: Multitask data augmentation approach able to improve translation performance by generating synthetic training samples with non-fluent target segments (Sánchez-Cartagena et al., 2024).[5]

CrossLingualNeuralFMS: Method for obtaining translation proposal from target-language monolingual corpora in CAT tools (Esplà-Gomis et al., 2022).[6]

Tune 'n' distill: Pipeline to tune the mBART50 model to low-resource language pairs, and distill the resulting system to obtain a lightweight model (Galiano-Jiménez et al., 2023).[7]

PILAR: Collection of parallel and monolingual corpora for low-resource languages of the Iberian Peninsula.[8]

MayanV: Parallel corpora between several Mayan languages and Spanish (Lou et al., 2024).[9]

URL2lang: Tool to infer the language of a document from the URL linking to it.[10]

Parallel URLs Classifier: Tool to infer whether a pair of URLs link to parallel documents.[11]

Acknowledgments

Project (PID2021-127999NB-I00) funded by the Spanish Ministry of Science and Innovation, the Spanish Research Agency (AEI/10.13039/501100011033) and the European Regional Development Fund A way to make Europe.

References

Esplà-Gomis, M., V.M. Sánchez-Cartagena, J.A. Pérez-Ortiz, and F. Sánchez-Martínez. 2022. Cross-lingual neural fuzzy matching for exploiting target-language monolingual corpora in computer-aided translation. In *Proc. of the 2022 EMNLP Conference*, pages 7532–7543, December.

Galiano-Jiménez, A., F. Sánchez-Martínez, V.M. Sánchez-Cartagena, and J.A. Pérez-Ortiz. 2023. Exploiting large pre-trained models for low-resource neural machine translation. In *Proc. of the 24th EAMT Conference*, pages 59–68, June.

Lou, A., J.A. Pérez-Ortiz, F. Sánchez-Martínez, and V.M. Sánchez-Cartagena. 2024. Curated datasets and neural models for machine translation of informal registers between mayan and spanish vernaculars. In *Proc. of the 2024 NAACL Conference*, Mexico City, Mexico, June. In press.

Sánchez-Cartagena, V.M., M. Esplà-Gomis, J.A. Pérez-Ortiz, and F. Sánchez-Martínez. 2024. Non-fluent synthetic target-language data improve neural machine translation. *IEEE Transactions on Pattern Analysis and Machine Intelligence*, 46(2):837–850.

[4]For a complete list we refer the reader to `https://transducens.dlsi.ua.es/lilowla/lilowla-resources/`

[5]`https://github.com/transducens/MaTiLDA`

[6]`https://github.com/transducens/CrossLingualNeuralFMS`

[7]`https://github.com/transducens/tune-n-distill`

[8]`https://github.com/transducens/PILAR/`

[9]`https://github.com/transducens/mayanv`

[10]`https://github.com/transducens/url2lang`

[11]`https://github.com/transducens/parallel-urls-classifier`

MaTIAS: Machine Translation to Inform Asylum Seekers

Lieve Macken, Ella van Hest, Arda Tezcan, Michaël Lumingu, Katrijn Maryns and July De Wilde
Department of Translation, Interpreting and Communication
Ghent University
Belgium
{firstname.lastname}@ugent.be

Abstract

This project aims to develop a multilingual notification system for asylum reception centres in Belgium using machine translation. The system will allow staff to communicate practical messages to residents in their own language. Ethnographically inspired fieldwork is being conducted in reception centres to understand current communication practices and ensure that the technology meets user needs. The quality and suitability of machine translation will be evaluated for three MT systems supporting all target languages. Automatic and manual evaluation methods will be used to assess translation quality, and terms of use, privacy and data protection conditions will be analysed.

1 Project overview

Machine translation plays a key role in contexts of migration (Valdez et al., 2023; Vieira et al., 2021). Known problems with the use of MT in migration settings are related to translation quality, lack of domain-specific vocabulary and privacy concerns (Liebling et al., 2020).

This project aims to develop a prototype of a multilingual notification system tailored to asylum reception facilities. The project is being conducted in collaboration with Fedasil, the federal agency responsible for the provision of asylum reception in Belgium. The project is funded by AMIF, the EU Asylum Migration and Integration Fund, and started in July 2023 and will end in December 2025.

The notification system will allow reception centre staff to convey practical messages and instructions to centre residents in the latter's own languages. In doing so, the project aims to support the reception facilities in two main needs: rapid communication of practical information with residents (e.g. "the teacher is sick so there will be no Dutch classes today") and language support for minority languages.

The prototype will consist of a web platform that Fedasil employees can use to translate English, French or Dutch text messages into a set of at least 14 languages[1], including low-resourced languages such as Pashto, Somali and Tigrinya. The translations are either retrieved from a context-specific translation memory or generated by a machine translation (MT) system. These translations are then automatically sent using an existing messaging system (e.g. WhatsApp, Signal, Telegram).

2 Project phases

MaTIAS is an interdisciplinary project that combines methods from linguistic ethnography and translation technology research. The project is divided into four phases: (1) practice-oriented research comprising ethnographic fieldwork and the evaluation and selection of suitable MT systems; (2) content and product development; (3) training; and (4) user evaluation and satisfaction research. The activities and preliminary results of the first phase of the project are detailed below.

3 Ethnographic fieldwork

The ethnographic fieldwork at the reception centres aims to (1) understand the current communication practices and to make an inventory of

[1] All languages available at https://www.fedasilinfo.be/

Proceedings of the 25th Annual Conference of the European Association for Machine Translation (Volume 2), pages 6–7
June 24-27, 2024 ©2024 European Association for Machine Translation

the most common messages (announcements, instructions) in the reception facilities. This inventory, which consists of frequent phrases and their translations, forms one input source of the context-specific translation memory; (2) gain an insight into the necessary preconditions to optimally use the developed technology (e.g. required expertise among users, attitudes and trust among users, receptivity towards this technology, IT infrastructure, user security, etc.); and (3) gain an understanding of residents' communication preferences to determine which messaging system is best suited to link to the web platform.

So far, the fieldwork has yielded important insights on users' expectations and potential usage obstacles. Firstly, the participants have high expectations on translation accuracy. The staff believe the notification system will facilitate their communication practices significantly. Residents, on the other hand, expressed their support for the system but would prefer technology that allows two-way messaging. Secondly, low literacy in some residents has been identified as a major obstacle for the reception of messages in written form. Therefore, we will explore possibilities of using text-to-speech settings to enable the read-aloud function on different types of smartphones. Finally, the fieldwork data highlights the benefits of incorporating the source language text into the message, rather than simply presenting the translated version. This practice not only serves as an invaluable resource for residents seeking more detailed information from staff, but also provides an excellent opportunity for residents to familiarise themselves with the local language.

4 MT evaluation

We will test the quality and suitability of three different MT systems that support all target languages: two commercial engines (ModernMT and Google Translate), which both allow for some degree of customisation and one open-source model (Meta AI's *No Language Left Behind*-model). For each of these systems, we will also evaluate the impact of the source language on translation quality, in particular English versus Dutch or French for translation into the minority languages.

We will use both automatic and manual evaluation methods to assess MT quality. As a first step, MT quality will be assessed using reference-based automatic evaluation metrics such as BLEU, TER, chrF, BLEURT, BERTscore and COMET. Translation memories linked to www.fedasilinfo.be were obtained from Fedasil for all languages except Dutch, French, German and Spanish, from which we extracted reference translations. In addition, to create a test set, we identified 43 web pages from www.fedasilinfo.be that were most relevant to our project[2] and extracted and sentence aligned all textual information for the missing languages.

From this set, we collected all sentences for which translations are available in all 14 languages. The resulting test set of 577 sentences will be used for all automatic evaluations. Based on the results of the automatic evaluations, a decision will be taken as to which MT systems will be manually evaluated by language experts.

In addition to assessing the MT quality, a thorough analysis of the terms of use for the three different MT systems will be conducted to gain a comprehensive understanding of the privacy and data protection conditions. Furthermore, factors such as deployment features and the ease of integration into the web platform will be taken into consideration. Based on the results obtained from these evaluations, a final decision on which engines to integrate will be made in consultation with Fedasil.

Acknowledgements: This project is co-financed by the European Commission under the Asylum, Migration and Integration Fund (AMIF 093-133).

References

Liebling, Daniel J, Michal Lahav, Abigail Evans, Aaron Donsbach, Jess Holbrook, Boris Smus, and Lindsey Boran. 2020. Unmet needs and opportunities for mobile translation AI. In *Proceedings of the 2020 CHI conference on human factors in computing systems*, pages 1–13.

Valdez, Susana, Ana Guerberof Arenas, and Kars Ligtenberg. 2023. Migrant communities living in the Netherlands and their use of MT in healthcare settings. In *Proceedings of the 24th Annual Conference of the European Association for Machine Translation*, pages 325–334, Tampere, Finland, June. European Association for Machine Translation.

Vieira, Lucas Nunes, Minako O'Hagan, and Carol O'Sullivan. 2021. Understanding the societal impacts of machine translation: a critical review of the literature on medical and legal use cases. *Information, Communication & Society*, 24(11):1515–1532.

[2]e.g. https://www.fedasilinfo.be/en/your-stay-reception-place

SmartBiC: Smart Harvesting of Bilingual Corpora from the Internet

Gema Ramírez-Sánchez, Sergio Ortiz-Rojas, Alicia Núñez Alcover, Tudor N. Mateiu, Mikel L. Forcada
Prompsit Language Engineering
info@prompsit.com

Pedro L. Díez Orzas, Almudena Ballester Carrillo, Giuseppe Deriard Nolasco, Noelia Jiménez Listón
Linguaserve Int. de Servicios
clientes@linguaserve.com

Abstract

SmartBiC, an 18-month innovation project funded by the Spanish Government, aims at improving the full process of collecting, filtering and selecting in-domain parallel content to be used for machine translation and language model tuning purposes in industrial settings. Based on state-of-the-art technology in the free/open-source parallel web corpora harvester Bitextor, SmartBic develops a web-based application around it including novel components such as a language -and domain- focused crawler and a domain-specific corpora selector. SmartBic also addresses specific industrial use cases for individual components of the Bitextor pipeline, such as parallel data cleaning. Relevant improvements to the current Bitextor pipeline will be publicly released.

1 Introduction

Obtaining a suitable amount of parallel corpora to train neural machine translation (NMT) or large language models (LLMs) is a challenging task, which becomes particularly difficult for domain-specific areas. This is seen as a severe limitation for the full development of NMT and LLMs in industrial settings. SmartBic, an innovation project ending in September 2023 with support from the Spanish Government through the NextGenerationEU funds, addresses this limitation from an industrial perspective. The main goal of SmartBiC is to ease the collection, filtering and selection of in-domain parallel corpora by exploring multilingual websites and external corpora. To that end, SmartBiC builds upon Bitextor,[1] a free/open-source parallel corpora harvester, adding the following improved and novel components described in detail in section 3: a smart crawler, a smart cleaner, and a smart corpora selector. In-domain corpora produced with SmartBiC will be used in industrial use cases, particularly to train domain-specific NMT systems, but also to explore their usefulness as LLM training or tuning datasets. This will extrinsically evaluate the quality and usefulness of the results of the project and point to improvements for future work.

2 Bitextor as the core technology

Bitextor (Espla-Gomis et al., 2016) has been used to produce petabytes of parallel corpora from multilingual web-crawled content in previous EU-funded projects such as `ParaCrawl.eu` or `MaCoCu.eu`. Among other alternatives, such as the ILSP-FC focused crawler (Papavassiliou et al., 2013), Bitextor is chosen for its language support, active developer community and modular design.

3 New components in SmartBiC

SmartBiC addresses the following limitations in Bitextor in order to achieve the goals of the project: (1) crawlers in Bitextor download websites ignoring the language pair indicated in the input, only a tiny portion of the crawled content makes it to the output, (2) no topic or domain constraints are currently handled by Bitextor, in-domain and generic content is mixed in the output parallel corpus and (3) seed URLs need to be manually provided to the crawler and no mechanism to automatically discover further interesting URLs is available.

[1] `https://github.com/bitextor/bitextor`

Proceedings of the 25th Annual Conference of the European Association for Machine Translation (Volume 2), pages 8–9
June 24-27, 2024 ©2024 European Association for Machine Translation

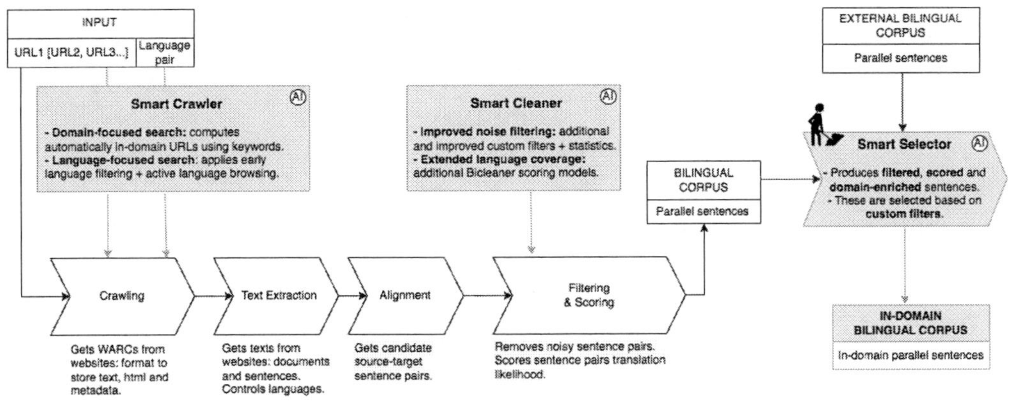

Figure 1: Bitextor pipeline (uncoloured boxes) and new and enhanced components provided by SmartBiC (coloured boxes).

SmartBiC adds as new components to Bitextor to overcome these limitations (see Figure 1):

The **Smart Crawler** module which improves the current generic crawler by integrating both language pair and domain focus during crawling and includes: (1) two new crawlers with complementary crawling strategies which filter content by language pair, reducing the amount of information downloaded; (2) a mechanism to automatically find URLs from another URL, a text or a keyword list Exploiting these keywords, potentially similar URLs are discovered using browser-based queries.

The **Smart Cleaner**, a stand-alone component that enhances and provides the functionality of the Bitextor cleaning pipeline; it includes: (1) improved and new filters with customisable thresholds; (2) support for new language pairs, that is, new models for Bicleaner; (3) custom filtering, cleaning statistics and new output formats.

The **Smart Selector** independent module which picks the most relevant set of in-domain data from already crawled or generic corpora and includes: (1) a separate, standalone cleaning step to filter out noisy sentence pairs and to score the remaining ones with Bicleaner (Zaragoza-Bernabeu et al., 2022); (2) a multilingual zero-shot classifier which adds domain scores to each sentence in a sentence pair; (3) a customisable sentence pair selector based on size, domain, cleaning scores and content quality.

Relevant components resulting from this project will be released through Bitextor.

3.1 SmartBiC web application

SmartBiC will be operated mainly by computational linguists and translators through a web application developed within the project. The main features of this web application, which adds usability to current command-line-only Bitextor, will allow users to launch and monitor crawling, cleaning and in-domain data selection tasks.

3.2 Acknowledgements

SmartBiC is funded by NextGenerationEU funds of the Spanish Government through the grants for Artificial Intelligence Research and Development projects and other digital technologies and their implementation in value chains (C005/21-ED) by "Entidad Pública Empresarial RED.ES, M.P.", grant number 2021/C005/00150077.

References

Espla-Gomis, Miquel, Mikel L Forcada, Sergio Ortiz-Rojas, and Jorge Ferrández-Tordera. 2016. Bitextor's participation in wmt'16: shared task on document alignment. In *Proceedings of the First Conference on Machine Translation: Volume 2, Shared Task Papers*, pages 685–691.

Papavassiliou, Vassilis, Prokopis Prokopidis, and Gregor Thurmair. 2013. A modular open-source focused crawler for mining monolingual and bilingual corpora from the web. In *Proceedings of the Sixth Workshop on Building and Using Comparable Corpora*, pages 43–51, Sofia, Bulgaria, August. Association for Computational Linguistics.

Zaragoza-Bernabeu, Jaume, Gema Ramírez-Sánchez, Marta Bañón, and Sergio Ortiz Rojas. 2022. Bicleaner AI: Bicleaner goes neural. In *Proceedings of the Thirteenth Language Resources and Evaluation Conference*, pages 824–831, Marseille, France, June. European Language Resources Association.

An Eye-Tracking Study on the Use of Machine Translation Post-Editing and Automatic Speech Recognition in Translations for the Medical Domain

Raluca Chereji
Human and Artificial Intelligence in Translation (HAITrans) research group
Centre for Translation Studies
University of Vienna
raluca-maria.chereji@univie.ac.at

Abstract

This EAMT-funded eye-tracking study investigates the impact of Machine Translation Post-Editing and Automatic Speech Recognition on English–Romanian translations of medical texts for patients. This paper provides an overview of the study objectives, setup and preliminary results.

1 Project Overview

Research in the medical domain indicates that medical texts for patients, such as patient information leaflets (PILs) and informed consent forms (ICFs), are too complex to be understood by their lay target audience, due to linguistic features such as medical jargon or syntactic complexity (Terblanche and Burgess, 2010). In some cases, medical translators can replicate and/or exacerbate these comprehensibility issues through their translation choices (Montalt et al., 2018). Given the technologisation seen across the broader translation industry (ELIA et al., 2023), it is worth considering whether and how could existing technologies be leveraged to support medical translators in producing more readable and lay-friendly translations of medical texts for patients.

The present study aims to address this research gap by investigating the impact of Machine Translation Post-Editing (MTPE), dictated translation using an Automatic Speech Recognition (ASR) tool and standard typed translation in the context of ICF translations from English into Romanian (EN–RO). The study draws on prior research on translation modalities (Daems et al., 2017; Guerberof Arenas et al., 2021) and measures this impact across four variables: (1) output quality, readability and lay-friendliness; (2) cognitive load, measured using an eye-tracker; (3) task productivity; and (4) participants' self-reported perceptions.

The main objective of this study is to assess whether MTPE, dictated translation using ASR or typed translation has a significant effect on participating translators' **product** and **process** and would thus lend itself better to patient-facing medical translation workflows. More specifically, we are interested in finding out which condition produces the most readable and lay-friendly translation, and how it impacts translators' speed, cognitive load and preferences compared to the other conditions. These results will help inform guidelines and training materials on MTPE and ASR for medical translators working on patient-facing medical texts.

2 Study Design and Methodology

Data collection took place in March 2023 in Cluj-Napoca, Romania, and forms part of a three-year doctoral project (2022–2025) at the University of Vienna Centre for Translation Studies. Seven participants, all professional medical translators, performed three EN–RO translation tasks using the Computer-Assisted Translation (CAT) tool Matecat:[1] **(1) typed translation from scratch**, still the dominant way to translate (ELIA et al., 2023); **(2) MTPE**, for which the raw output was generated using an MBart model (Liu et al., 2020) fine-tuned for the medical domain using the EN–RO dataset of the European Medicines Agency parallel corpus (ELG, 2020); **(3) dictated translation from scratch** using the dictation function in Matecat which uses the Google Speech-to-Text API.[2]

[1] https://www.matecat.com/
[2] https://cloud.google.com/speech-to-text

Proceedings of the 25th Annual Conference of the European Association for Machine Translation (Volume 2), pages 10–11
June 24-27, 2024 ©2024 European Association for Machine Translation

The source texts were three ICF excerpts (956 words) from the United States National Library of Medicine clinical trials database.[3] Comparability was checked using readability formulae, and linguistic complexity and lexical richness metrics. We commissioned a gold standard translation of the source texts by two professional EN–RO medical translators who, like the participating translators, were given explicit guidelines to ensure their translations were readable and lay-friendly within the constraints of the ICF text genre.

During the tasks, participants' eye movements were recorded using an EyeLink Portable Duo eye tracker,[4] with their on-screen behaviour and keystrokes recorded in the WebLink software.[5] Participants also filled out pre- and post-task questionnaires on their MTPE and ASR experience and in-task performance. They were compensated for their participation, which took up to 3 hours.

3 Analysis and Future Work

The study data (eye-tracking video recordings, keystroke- and time-logging, questionnaires, and target translations) are currently undergoing statistical analysis (including regression modeling). Preliminary results suggest:

- **Cognitive load** (mean fixation durations in the source and target texts): there are no statistically significant differences in participants' cognitive load in the three conditions.
- **Productivity** (total task time in minutes): post-editing was about twice as fast as typing. Dictation was also faster than typing, in line with other studies (Ciobanu, 2016).
- **Self-reported perceptions** (pre- and post-task questionnaires): Participants' preferred working condition varied, but 5 out of 7 participants disliked MTPE the most.

These results suggest that MTPE and ASR do not hinder the translation process from a cognitive standpoint, are faster than typed translation, and there is openness to their adoption among our study participants, though this is more limited for MTPE. In future work, we will measure the effect of MTPE, ASR and typed translation on output quality and lay-friendliness by assessing participants' translations against the gold standard using a customised annotation typology. The eye-tracking videos, target translations and questionnaire templates will be published on PHAIDRA[6] under a CC BY 4.0 International license once the author's doctoral project is completed.

4 Acknowledgements

This project was funded through the EAMT 2023 Sponsorship of Activities program (project 5369). The author thanks Dr Miguel Angel Ríos Gaona for fine-tuning the MBart engine and assisting with statistical data analysis.

References

Ciobanu, Dragoş. 2016. Automatic Speech Recognition in the professional translation process. *Translation Spaces*, 5(1):124–144.

Daems, Joke, Sonia Vandepitte, Robert Hartsuiker, and Lieve Macken. 2017. Translation methods and experience: A comparative analysis of human translation and post-editing with students and professional translators. *Meta*, 62(2):245–270.

ELG. 2020. ELG - Bilingual corpus made out of PDF documents from the European Medicines Agency, (EMEA), https://www.ema.europa.eu, (February 2020) (EN-RO).

ELIA, EMT, EUATC, FIT EUROPE, GALA, LIND, and WOMEN IN LOCALIZATION. 2023. 2023 European Language Industry Survey. Trends, expectations and concerns of the European language industry. Technical report.

Guerberof Arenas, Ana, Joss Moorkens, and Sharon O'Brien. 2021. The impact of translation modality on user experience: an eye-tracking study of the microsoft word user interface. *Machine Translation*, 35(2):205–237.

Liu, Yinhan, Jiatao Gu, Naman Goyal, Xian Li, Sergey Edunov, Marjan Ghazvininejad, Mike Lewis, and Luke Zettlemoyer. 2020. Multilingual denoising pre-training for neural machine translation. *Transactions of the Association for Computational Linguistics*, 8:726–742.

Montalt, Vicent, Karen Korning Zethsen, and Wioleta Karwacka. 2018. Medical translation in the 21st century - challenges and trends. *MonTI. Monografías de Traducción e Interpretación*, (10):27–42.

Terblanche, Marli and Lesley Burgess. 2010. Examining the readability of patient-informed consent forms. *Open Access Journal of Clinical Trials*, 2:157–162, October. Dove Press.

[3]https://clinicaltrials.gov/
[4]https://www.sr-research.com/eyelink-portable-duo/
[5]https://www.sr-research.com/weblink/
[6]https://phaidra.univie.ac.at/

The MAKE-NMTViz Project: Meaningful, Accurate and Knowledge-limited Explanations of NMT Systems for Translators

Gabriela Gonzalez-Saez[1], Fabien Lopez[1], Mariam Nakhle[1 5], Marco Dinarelli[1], Emmanuelle Esperança-Rodier[1], Sui He[4], Caroline Rossi[2], Didier Schwab[1], Jun Yang[4], James Robert Turner[4], Nicolas Ballier[3]

1 Univ. Grenoble Alpes, CNRS, Grenoble INP, LIG 38000 Grenoble, France
2 Université Grenoble Alpes
3 Université Paris Cité, LLF & CLILLAC-ARP, 75013 Paris, France
4 Swansea University
5 Lingua Custodia, France
Contact: gabriela-nicole.gonzalez-saez@univ-grenoble-alpes.fr

Abstract

This paper describes MAKE-NMTViz, a project designed to help translators visualize neural machine translation outputs using explainable artificial intelligence visualization tools initially developed for computer vision.

1 Introduction

In their meta-review Doran et al. (2017) distinguish opaque, interpretable, and comprehensible systems across various fields including computer vision and natural language processing. Neural machine translation (NMT) falls into the category of comprehensible systems, provided that adequate visualisation systems are implemented. They argue that "confidence in an interpretable learning system is a function of the user's ability to understand the machine's input/output mapping behaviour". Following the NIST report on Explainable Artificial Intelligence (XAI) (Phillips et al., 2021), we will explore their four principles of XAI, which we have rearranged to spell out our MAKE paradigm:

Meaningfulness We want our visualisation system to be understandable and comprehensible to the translator, putting meaning back at the heart of the NMT process.

Accuracy: Our system will improve our understanding of the input-process-output mapping. It may also identify aspects that are not visually apparent by utilizing visualizations that demonstrate the NMT system's internal working.

Knowledge Limits: The visualizations will be limited to the NMT system's knowledge, operating only under conditions for which it was designed and when it reaches sufficient confidence in its output, thus revealing to the user the uncertainties inherent in the results. This will be achieved by including different metrics, such as confidence and quality estimation for MT.

Explanation: We hope to provide visual evidence of the workings of the different steps (subtokenisation/encoding/decoding), thus accounting e.g. for some NMT hallucinations on the basis of the frequencies of the subtokens.

In this project, we propose to develop a platform that offers meaningful, accurate, and knowledge-limited explanations of NMT systems for translators. While current neural network visualization primarily focuses on analyzing activation patterns for classification tasks, our project expands its scope to investigate the effects of linguistic structures and neural representations. Through our platform, translators will have the capability to translate, post-edit, and evaluate while simultaneously analyzing and explaining NMT model results, thereby bridging the gap between complex Artificial Intelligence (AI) algorithms and human understanding in translation.

2 Expected Results

We intend to develop and utilize a Python-based system that leverages state-of-the-art tools to provide a comprehensive approach for analyzing input, process, and output in NMT. We draw inspiration from the *seq2seqVis* system (Strobelt et al., 2018), adapting its functionalities to analyze the decision-making process of NMT systems. We incorporate attribution methods for feature importance explanations from the *Inseq* System (Sarti et al., 2023) (e.g. saliency maps), enabling interoperability with FairSeq (Ott et al., 2019) models for analyzing relationships between NMT model components. Furthermore, we integrate

Proceedings of the 25th Annual Conference of the European Association for Machine Translation (Volume 2), pages 12–13
June 24-27, 2024 ©2024 European Association for Machine Translation

attention weight analysis strategies based on BertViz visualization (Vig, 2019), and other methods that attempt to inspect the model's internal data, thus enabling a comprehensive visualization of the data cycle for NMT. Our platform supports FairSeq models with the addition of unobtrusive probes, called *decorators*, to traceable parts of the NMT architecture, enabling flexible integration across various NMT architectures.

3 Visualiser

The visualizer is composed of four interoperable modules: translation, analysis, post-editing, and evaluation.

The *translation* module is responsible for loading the model and source text, generating the translated text, and storing the internal data of the system's working (e.g., attention weights, sequence generation probabilities). Once the translation is completed, the *analysis* module steps in to explain how the NMT model arrives at the proposed translation. The explanation comprises three parts: input, process and output, guiding the user process the system took to create the translation step-by-step (or token-by-token). The input analysis focuses on its representation and the sub-tokenization used. The process describes the workings of the model and its interaction with the input, connecting the model's internal data and features to the output. Finally, the output displays in the target language all the different alternatives the model generates and explains why it chose the final proposed translation.

To give the translation control to the translator we incorporate a *post-editing* module, which gives the translator the possibility to use other alternatives proposed by the NMT system, but also to force the generation of specific tokens to update the analysis module. The *evaluation* module complements the post-editing module. A post-edited text serves as the ground truth, enabling evaluation of the initially generated proposal. This reference can be replaced by standard datasets to conduct stand-alone evaluations. The evaluation contextualise the explanation of the analysis module.

4 Conclusion

In this project, we propose to change the perspective of current explainability tools and systems which do not target the translator audience. Instead, we explore the use of these systems in the translation pipeline. While existing systems are too complex to be installed and too experimental to reach the corpus linguistics and translation studies communities, our system intends to be user-centred, for a genuinely human-centred AI, and intends to add functionalities and serve as an all-in-one wrapper. The visualising tool current functionalities can be tested on Hugging Face Spaces.[1]

5 The Funding Body and Consortium

This project emanated from research supported by the MAKE-NMTVIZ project (14 months since November 2023), funded under the 2022 Grenoble-Swansea Centre for AI Call for Proposals/ GoSCAI - Grenoble-Swansea Joint Centre in Human Centred AI and Data Systems (MIAI@Grenoble Alpes (ANR-19-P3IA-0003)). This work was also supported by the CREMA project (**co**reference **re**solution into **ma**chine translation) funded by the French National Research Agency (ANR), contract number ANR-21-CE23-0021-01.
The Consortium comprises AI specialists from GETALP@UGA, linguistic experts Caroline Rossi and Nicolas Ballier (NMT specialists), and Jun Yang, Sui He and James Robert Turner, all from the Swansea Translation and Interpreting Group (STING). Its goal is to develop translation tools that integrate both linguistic and AI perspectives, fostering collaboration between translators and specialists in the field.

References

Doran, D, SC Schulz, and TR Besold. 2017. What does explainable ai really mean? a new conceptualization of perspectives. In *First International Workshop on Comprehensibility and Explanation in AI and ML 2017, CEUR Workshop Proceedings, Vol. 2071.*

Ott, Myle, Sergey Edunov, Alexei Baevski, Angela Fan, Sam Gross, Nathan Ng, David Grangier, and Michael Auli. 2019. fairseq: A fast, extensible toolkit for sequence modeling. In *NAACL-HLT 2019*, pages 48–53.

Phillips, P. Jonathon, Carina Hahn, Peter Fontana, Amy Yates, Kristen K. Greene, David Broniatowski, and Mark A. Przybocki. 2021. Four principles of explainable artificial intelligence, https://doi.org/10.6028/nist.ir.8312.

Sarti, Gabriele, Nils Feldhus, Ludwig Sickert, and Oskar van der Wal. 2023. Inseq: An interpretability toolkit for sequence generation models. In *Proc. of 61st Meeting of the Association for Computational Linguistics*, pages 421–435.

Strobelt, Hendrik, Sebastian Gehrmann, Michael Behrisch, Adam Perer, Hanspeter Pfister, and Alexander M Rush. 2018. Seq2seq-vis: A visual debugging tool for sequence-to-sequence models. *IEEE Transactions on Visualization and Computer Graphics*, 25(1):353–363.

Vig, Jesse. 2019. A multiscale visualization of attention in the transformer model. In *Proc. of 57th Meeting of the Association for Computational Linguistics*, pages 37–42.

[1] `https://huggingface.co/gabrielanicole`

MULTILINGTOOL, Development of an Automatic Multilingual Subtitling and Dubbing System

Ander Corral[1], Xabier Sarasola[1], Iker Manterola[2], Josu Murua[2], Itziar Cortes[2], Igor Leturia[1], Xabier Saralegi[1]
[1]Orai NLP Technologies/Elhuyar
{a.corral,x.sarasola,i.leturia,x.saralegi}@orai.eus
[2]Elhuyar Foundation
{i.manterola,j.murua,i.cortes}@elhuyar.eus

Abstract

In this paper, we present the MULTILINGTOOL project, led by the Elhuyar Foundation and funded by the European Commission under the CREA-MEDIA2022-INNOVBUSMOD call. The aim of the project is to develop an advanced platform for automatic multilingual subtitling and dubbing. It will provide support for Spanish, English, and French, as well as the co-official languages of Spain, namely Basque, Catalan, and Galician.

1 Introduction

Over the past two decades, the European audiovisual industry has undergone significant transformation due to advancements in information and communication technologies and shifts in consumer behavior, leading to a market predominantly controlled by a few large corporations. These changes have raised concerns regarding the sustainability of content production by European entities and the maintenance of the continent's cultural diversity. However, artificial intelligence (AI) provides a promising solution for smaller firms, enabling them to access enhanced subtitling and dubbing services in various languages. This technology helps expand their reach and visibility across Europe, thus bolstering the industry's diversity and resilience.

The MULTILINGTOOL project (CREA-PJG/101093511), led by the Elhuyar Foundation and financed by the CREA-MEDIA2022-INNOVBUSMOD call, commenced in 2022 and is scheduled to conclude in March 2025. Its primary objective is to develop an innovative automatic subtitling and dubbing platform specifically designed for the audiovisual sector. This platform can perform **automatic dubbing in multiple languages**, including English, French, Spanish, Basque, Galician, and Catalan. It integrates three core technologies: Automatic Speech Recognition (ASR), Machine Translation (MT), and Text-to-Speech (TTS). The platform also features **customizable dubbing voices**, allowing users to tailor the voices to enhance their final audiovisual content. Additionally, it includes a web-based interface that enables both users and content companies to efficiently **manage and review** multilingual audiovisual content, which includes subtitles, translations, and dubbing.

2 Platform specifications

A modular architecture has been developed to support multilingual transcription, neural machine translation, and personalized speech synthesis use cases. Emphasizing modularity is key to achieving robust and easily adaptable software.

2.1 ASR module

We have fine-tuned Whisper-based (Radford et al., 2023) systems for all languages involved in the project, except for English as it already obtains competitive enough results. Data augmentation techniques have been used to enhance the adaptability and robustness of the ASR module against a diverse range of acoustic phenomena encountered in real-world scenarios, such as speed and volume perturbations and a diverse set of out-of-speech signals and artifacts, including music, background noise, chatter, telephone codecs, and reverberation. We opted for the small version of Whisper to

Proceedings of the 25th Annual Conference of the European Association for Machine Translation (Volume 2), pages 14–15
June 24-27, 2024 ©2024 European Association for Machine Translation

strike a balance between performance and resource utilization. We tested our fine-tuned systems on the FLEURS standard benchmark (Conneau et al., 2022). The quality of the transcriptions has been measured in terms of word error rates (WER) as shown in Table 1.

Language	FLEURS
es	7.31
en	6.53
fr	12.37
ca	10.75
gl	14.49
eu	15.34

Table 1: WER results of the Whisper-based fine-tuned systems for the multilingual ASR module.

2.2 NMT module

A multilingual NMT module involving the six languages of the project was developed. Due to the lack of sufficient volume of training samples for some of the translation directions, a Spanish-centric pivoted translation approach has been considered, where translating from one language to another is done via Spanish. Systems were trained using the Transformer (Vaswani et al., 2017) base architecture. Data augmentation techniques were applied for general system robustness against ASR module's casing and punctuation errors and input perturbations. Additionally, we adapted the systems for an informal/speaking register leveraging back-translation for more in-domain data. All the systems were evaluated on the Flores200 test set by using the BLEU metric as reported in Table 2.

2.3 TTS module

A multispeaker cross-lingual speech synthesis system has been created to use custom speakers for dubbing in multiple languages. Our system is based on Fastpitch (Łańcucki, 2021) and we added a language embedding to make a multispeaker multilingual Fastpitch. The language embedding is added to the input of the encoder similar to the speaker embedding in the multispeaker Fastpitch. To evaluate the model we selected 30 sentences in English and we synthesized them with speakers with recordings in different languages in a cross-lingual way. For the English speaker, we translated the 30 sentences to French and we made the cross-lingual synthesis in French. We evaluated the resulting speech with neural network based Mean Opinion Score (MOS) and Speaker Encoder Cosine Similarity (SECS). The results are shown in Table 3.

	Flores200	
Language pair	→	←
es-en	26.7	24.9
es-fr	26.3	22.8
es-gl	13.4	18.3
es-ca	22.7	24.1
es-eu	21.6	23.6

Table 2: BLEU scores for all the translation directions developed for the multilingual NMT module.

lang	ref	cross-lingual voice (en*)	
	MOS	MOS	SECS
ca	3.21±0.11	3.82±0.09	0.39
es	4.11±0.08	4.20±0.05	0.36
en	4.36±0.04	3.46±0.16	0.59
eu	3.42±0.11	3.95±0.08	0.35
fr	3.13±0.03	3.90±0.07	0.33
gl	3.84±0.10	4.15±0.07	0.68

Table 3: MOS and SECS scores of the multispeaker cross-lingual speech synthesis system. *The English speaker synthesized French sentences.

References

Conneau, Alexis, Min Ma, Simran Khanuja, Yu Zhang, Vera Axelrod, Siddharth Dalmia, Jason Riesa, Clara Rivera, and Ankur Bapna. 2022. Fleurs: Few-shot learning evaluation of universal representations of speech. *arXiv preprint arXiv:2205.12446*.

Łańcucki, Adrian. 2021. Fastpitch: Parallel text-to-speech with pitch prediction. In *ICASSP 2021-2021 IEEE International Conference on Acoustics, Speech and Signal Processing (ICASSP)*, pages 6588–6592. IEEE.

Radford, Alec, Jong Wook Kim, Tao Xu, Greg Brockman, Christine McLeavey, and Ilya Sutskever. 2023. Robust speech recognition via large-scale weak supervision. In *International Conference on Machine Learning*, pages 28492–28518. PMLR.

Vaswani, Ashish, Noam Shazeer, Niki Parmar, Jakob Uszkoreit, Llion Jones, Aidan N Gomez, Łukasz Kaiser, and Illia Polosukhin. 2017. Attention is all you need. *Advances in neural information processing systems*, 30.

ERC Advanced Grant Project CALCULUS: Extending the Boundary of Machine Translation

Jingyuan Sun, Mingxiao Li, Ruben Cartuyvels and Marie-Francine Moens
Department of Computer Science, KU Leuven, Belgium
{jingyuan.sun, mingxiao.li, ruben.cartuyvels, sien.moens}@kuleuven.be

1 Fact Sheet

- **Project Acronym:** CALCULUS
- **Grant Agreement ID:** 788506
- **DOI:** https://doi.org/10.3030/788506
- **Funding Agency:** European Research Council (ERC) under the EXCELLENT SCIENCE programme
- **Duration:** Start Date: 1 September 2018 - End Date: 30 September 2024
- **Principle Investigator:** Prof. Dr. Marie-Francine Moens
- **Coordinator:** Katholieke Universiteit Leuven, Belgium

2 Objective

The CALCULUS project, drawing on human capabilities of imagination and commonsense for natural language understanding (NLU), aims to advance machine-based NLU by integrating traditional AI concepts with contemporary machine learning techniques. It focuses on developing anticipatory event representations from both textual and visual data, connecting language structure to visual spatial organization and incorporating broad knowledge domains. Anticipatory event representations refer to representations that are able to predict what content is highly probable to be communicated next in a discourse. CALCULUS tests these models in NLU tasks and uses real-world metrics to evaluate their ability to predict untrained spatial and temporal details. CALCULUS employs machine learning methods, including Bayesian techniques and artificial neural networks, especially in data-sparse scenarios. The project's culmination involves the interdisciplinary studies in natural language processing, visual data analysis and cognitive neuroscience

3 Relation with Machine Translation

In the CALCULUS project, we are broadening the horizons of machine translation by delving into the essence of transforming the formats of data distribution while keeping the meaning. This innovative approach involves converting information from one modality into another, transcending traditional linguistic boundaries. Our project includes novel work on translating text into images, videos and layouts and brain signals to stimuli as illustrated below. The proposed models for multimodal translation can be a source of inspiration for future language translation (e.g., noise reduction in diffusion models, loss functions that preserve the structure of the source input).

3.1 Text to Image/Video Translation

Creating images and videos from text, which can also be seen as translating text into visual signals, is a key aspect of advancing artificial-intelligence-generated content (AIGC), with diffusion models standing out for their effectiveness. However, these models face the challenge of exposure bias, which refers to the training inference discrepancy. To address this, we introduce the time shift sampler (Li et al., 2024), a novel sampling method that reduces bias without needing to retrain the model and can be seamlessly integrated into existing algorithms like denoising diffusion

Proceedings of the 25th Annual Conference of the European Association for Machine Translation (Volume 2), pages 16–17
June 24-27, 2024 ©2024 European Association for Machine Translation

probabilistic model (DDPM) and denoising diffusion implicit model (DDIM), enhancing text-to-image translation efficiency with minimal computational increase. On the other hand, converting text to videos is more complex due to the larger output space, demanding more sophisticated models to generate natural videos. We propose the scene and motion conditional diffusion (SMCD) approach, incorporating scene semantics, motion dynamics, and textual information to improve text-to-video translation. Specifically, we leverage the first frame as semantic conditioning and the sequence of bounding box of objects as motion dynamic conditioning. The diffusion UNet incorporates both semantic and motion dynamic conditioning via gated self-attention and cross-attention layers. SMCD employs an advanced motion conditioning module and various scene integration methods, fostering synergy between modalities for dynamic and coherent video generation that aligns with the input text and motion dynamics.

3.2 Text to Layout Translation

Translating text into a 2D spatial layout involves understanding both language and spatial organization, a crucial step in text-to-image synthesis that allows for precise and controlled image generation. Our study (Nuyts et al., 2024) reveals that layouts can be predicted from language representations that incorporate sentence syntax, whether implicitly or explicitly, especially when sentences describe entity relationships similar to those encountered during training. We add explicit syntax by encoding a sentence "*John hits the ball*" with its constituent structure marked by brackets: "*(S (NP John) (VP hits (NP the ball)))*".

However, when testing models with grammatically correct sentences describing novel combinations of known entities and relations, we observe a significant drop in performance. This decline indicates that current models mainly rely on training data correlations instead of on a disentangled understanding of the structural complexity of input sentences. To address this challenge, we introduce a novel contrastive loss function that pulls 2D-layout representations towards an encoding of the syntax of the sentence they depict. Hence, the syntactic structure of input sentences is retained more effectively in the outputs, especially when structure was already explicitly present in the input sentences (cf. the example above). Our approach demonstrates marked improvements in predicting 2D spatial layouts from textual descriptions.

3.3 Brain Signals to Image Translation

We delve into the groundbreaking task of translating brain signals into images (Sun et al., 2023a; Sun et al., 2023b). This task is notably complex due to the noisy nature of fMRI (functional magnetic resonance imaging) brain signals and the sophisticated visual patterns they represent. Our methodology introduces a two-phase framework for fMRI data representation learning. Initially, we use a double-contrastive mask auto-encoder to pre-train a feature learner, effectively extracting representations by denoising data, since the noises inherent in fMRI will severely influence the reconstruction quality. The subsequent phase fine-tunes this learner, honing in on neural activation patterns vital for visual reconstruction, guided by an image auto-encoder. Our approach has demonstrated exceptional capability, significantly surpassing existing models in semantic classification accuracy. We believe that such technology will be highly useful in the future when multi-modal translation is expected to conduct directly on human's brain signals to ensure seamless and real-time experiences.

References

Li, Mingxiao, Tingyu Qu, Ruicong Yao, Wei Sun, and Marie-Francine Moens. 2024. Alleviating exposure bias in diffusion models through sampling with shifted time steps. *International Conference on Learning Representations*.

Nuyts, Wolf, Ruben Cartuyvels, and Marie-Francine Moens. 2024. Explicitly representing syntax improves sentence-to-layout prediction of unexpected situations. *Transactions of the Association for Computational Linguistics*, 12:264–282.

Sun, Jingyuan, Mingxiao Li, Zijiao Chen, Yunhao Zhang, Shaonan Wang, and Marie-Francine Moens. 2023a. Contrast, attend and diffuse to decode high-resolution images from brain activities. In Oh, A., T. Neumann, A. Globerson, K. Saenko, M. Hardt, and S. Levine, editors, *Advances in Neural Information Processing Systems*, volume 36, pages 12332–12348. Curran Associates, Inc.

Sun, Jingyuan, Mingxiao Li, and Marie-Francine Moens. 2023b. Decoding realistic images from brain activity with contrastive self-supervision and latent diffusion. In *European Conference in Artificial Intelligence 2023*, volume Volume 372: ECAI 2023, pages 2250 – 2257.

GAMETRAPP project in progress: Designing a gamified environment for post-editing research abstracts

Cristina Toledo-Báez
Research Institute on Multilingual Language Technologies
University of Malaga
Spain
toledo@uma.es

Laura Noriega-Santiáñez
Research Institute on Multilingual Language Technologies
University of Malaga
Spain
laura.noriega@uma.es

Abstract

The «App for post-editing neural machine translation using gamification» (GAMETRAPP) project (TED2021-129789B-I00), funded by the Spanish Ministry of Science and Innovation (2022–2024), has been in progress for a year. Thus, this paper presents its main goals and the analysis of neural machine translation and post-editing errors of research abstracts carried out. This leads to the designing of the gamified environment, which is currently under construction.

1 Introduction

The era of artificial intelligence has undoubtedly shaped the evolution and refinement of language technologies, such as neural machine translation (NMT) systems, leading to the widespread adoption of post-editing (PE). Previous studies have explored the application of PE by scholars (Parra Escartín et al., 2017; Parra Escartín and Goulet, 2020; O'Brien et al., 2018) from a first language (L1) to a second language (L2) within academic contexts.

Against this background of scientific dissemination, the GAMETRAPP project aims to create a web application to bring closer the full PE of research abstracts following the IAMRaC structure,[1] in the Iberian Spanish→American English directionality, i.e., from a L1 to a L2. The potential users will be Spanish non-professional translators, specifically scholars.

Moreover, given the promising results of using gamification in non-professional contexts to enhance learning skills (Mahat et al., 2023), the GAMETRAPP app will feature a tailored-made gamified environment.

The GAMETRAPP team is made up by 23 scholars from both Spanish and American universities. Specifically, 7 universities from Spain (University of Malaga, University of Córdoba, University Pablo de Olavide, University of Alcalá, Complutense University of Madrid, University of Valladolid, and Valencia International University) and 2 from United States (Kent State University and Utah Valley University) (Toledo-Báez, 2023).

2 The GAMETRAPP project setup

After a year of its inception, the GAMETRAPP project is currently pursuing the following goals:

1. Analyze the NMT errors of research abstracts, specifically, those made by Google Translate in the Iberian Spanish→American English language combination.
2. Propose full PE guidelines to address the issues derived from the NMT output of research abstracts.
3. Study PE Literacy in the Spanish→English directionality in order to integrate these notions into the gamification.
4. Analyze the experience of Spanish scholars about NMT and PE knowledge and practice.
5. Create gamified activities to teach notions about PE of research abstracts presenting an IAMRaC structure to non-professional translators, specifically, scholars.

[1] This acronym stands for Introduction, Aims, Methodology, Results, and Conclusion. It is a variant of the IMRaD structure (i.e., Introduction, Methodology, Results, and Discussion).

Proceedings of the 25th Annual Conference of the European Association for Machine Translation (Volume 2), pages 18–20
June 24-27, 2024 ©2024 European Association for Machine Translation

6. Design an inclusive gamified environment to create an engaging, playful, and educational experience among users.
7. Develop a fully responsive web application to integrate the gamified environment.

3 NMT and PE analysis of research abstracts

To design the content of the gamified environment, four linguistic tasks have been carried out. First, the compilation of research abstracts that have been selected from 244 Spanish journals from the Q1 and Q2 in Scimago Journal & Country Rank in 2022. All abstracts have been manually analyzed and labelled considering their parts. Only 126 abstracts followed these three criteria: 1) published in 2023, 2) followed the IAMRaC structure, and 3) written by scholars affiliated with Spanish universities.

Second, Google Translate was chosen as the NMT system since it is widely used by scholars. Third, the selected abstracts were both human-translated into English by a professional translator having English as L1. They were also post-edited into English by a professional post-editor having English as L1.

Last, the fourth task consists of the linguistic analysis of the 126 machine-translated and post-edited research abstracts, using human translation as a gold standard. To carry out this task, the GAMETRAPP team in charge first focused on the resulting machine translation of the abstracts marking in bold red the NMT error, and then classified it based on the MQM (Multidimensional Quality Metrics)[2] errors typology (i.e., Terminology, Accuracy, Linguistic conventions, Style, Locale conventions, Audience appropriateness, Design and markup). Next, they focused on the post-editing of the abstracts marking in bold red the PE error and/or modifications in the segment under review. Once the PE error is identified, they assessed the PE based on the categories proposed by the Post-edit Me! Project[3] (i.e., value adding/successful edits, unnecessary edits, incomplete edits, or unsuccessful/error-introducing/missing edits). Finally, they added any key issues from the evaluation that they deemed pertinent.

This double analysis will not only help to determine several of the most frequent NMT errors for machine-translated research abstracts, but also to develop specific ES→EN PE guidelines of research abstracts and lay foundation for the gamified exercises.

4 The gamified environment

After carrying out the analysis, the gamified environment will be designed based on both the IAMRaC structure and the NMT and PE output. Thus, users will have to complete a series of activities within a gamified escape room experience divided into five levels. Each level represents each of the proposed IAMRaC parts of a research abstract. Users will play individually to unlock the levels, having three lives per level but not time limit.

The gamified activities are designed to train in PE through three stages: 1) the identification of NMT errors, i.e., those of Google Translate NMT system, 2) the practice of PE strategies in context, and 3) the pinpointing of PE errors. These activities are planned to be multiple choice (carried out by analyzing fuzzy matches different PE versions), gap-filling, and/or error correction. Lastly, a questionnaire will be created within the gamified activities to collect users' experiences, and thus test the usefulness of this technique. Thanks to the GAMETRAPP gamified environment, users should have learned full PE notions of research abstracts in the Iberian Spanish→American English language combination to help them post-edit their own academic productions.

Acknowledgments

This work has been carried out in the framework of several research projects: GAMETRAPP (TED2021-129789B-I00), NEUROTRAD (B1-2020_07), VIP II (PID2020-112818GB-I00), Proof-of-Concept VIP (PDC2021-121220-I00), RECOVER (ProyExcel_00540) and T2T (D5-2023_14).

References

Mahat, J., Alias N., and Yusop F. D. 2023. Systematic literature review on gamified professional training among employees. *Interactive Learning Environments*, 31(10):6747–6767.

O'Brien, S., Simard M., and Goulet M. 2018. Machine Translation and Self-Post-Editing for Academic Writing Support: Quality Explorations. In *Translation Quality Assessment. Machine Translation: Technologies and Applications* pages 237–262. Springer.

Parra Escartín, C., and Goulet M. J. 2020. When the Post-Editor is not a Translator: Can machine translation be post-edited by academics to prepare their publications in English? In *Translation Revision and Post-Editing* pages 89–106. Routledge.

Parra Escartín, Carla, Sharon O'Brien, Marie-Josée Goulet, and Michel Simard. 2017. Machine Translation as an Academic Writing Aid for Medical Practitioners. In *Proceedings of MT Summit XVI*, 254–267, Nagoya, Japan.

Toledo Báez, C. 2023. GAMETRAPP: Training app for post-editing neural machine translation using gamification in professional settings. In *Proceedings of the 24th*

[2] Available online at https://themqm.org/error-types-2/typology/.

[3] Available online at https://oer.uclouvain.be/jspui/handle/20.500.12279/829.

Annual Conference of the European Association for Machine Translation, pages 497–498, Tampere, Finland. European Association for Machine Translation.

RCnum: A Semantic and Multilingual Online Edition of the Geneva Council Registers from 1545 to 1550

Pierrette Bouillon[1], Christophe Chazalon[2], Sandra Coram-Mekkey[3], Gilles Falquet[2], Johanna Gerlach[1], Stéphane Marchand-Maillet[2], Laurent Moccozet[2], Jonathan Mutal[1], Raphael Rubino[1] and Marco Sorbi[2]

[1] TIM/FTI, University of Geneva, 1205 Geneva – Switzerland
`{firstName.lastName}@unige.ch`
[2] CUI, University of Geneva, 1205 Geneva – Switzerland
`{firstName.lastName}@unige.ch`
[3] Fondation de l'Encyclopédie de Genève
`coram.mekkey@gmail.com`

Abstract

The RCnum project is funded by the Swiss National Science Foundation and aims at producing a multilingual and semantically rich online edition of the Registers of Geneva Council from 1545 to 1550. Combining multilingual NLP, history and paleography, this collaborative project will clear hurdles inherent to texts manually written in 16th century Middle French while allowing for easy access and interactive consultation of these archives.

1 Introduction

The RCnum[1] project aims at producing a semantic and multilingual online edition of the Geneva Council Registers (*Registres du Conseil de Genève*, RC hereafter) for the years 1545 to 1550. This project, which began in July 2023 and will run until June 2027, is based on a synergy between the Fondation de l'Encyclopédie de Genève and two Geneva University faculties, namely the Centre universitaire d'informatique (CUI) and the Faculty of translation and interpreting (FTI). Previous work on RC have focused on manual transcription and editing, leading to in print publication for the years 1536 to 1544. Manual transcription from 1545 to 1550 has been conducted prior to this project, resulting in a digitised version of this corpus. RCnum's objective is to continue the digitisation effort while automatising RC modernisation, and to develop new functionalities to make RC accessible to a wide audience. RCnum is divided into four work packages (WP): 1) RC collection and preparation following Text Encoding Initiative guidelines, 2) automatic normalisation, modernisation and translation, 3) development of interactive and pedagogical exploration and visualisation tools, and 4) indexing, semantic enrichment and online platform development.

[1]`https://www.unige.ch/registresconseilge`

2 Project Description

Overview Comprising an uninterrupted series from 1409 until today, the RC document the work of the Geneva authorities, providing insights into society and politics over time. The RC in the time of Calvin, in particular, is an invaluable resource for the study of the political, legal, economic, social, and religious history of the Geneva region. These archives are also of philological interest, since they use Middle French for judicial and administrative matters which had until then been written in Latin. However, these documents remain difficult to understand for non-historians, paleographers, or experts in Middle French with knowledge of the political landscape during this period. Previous work in French modernisation has explored the use of machine translation (MT) approaches, including neural MT (e.g. Transformer (Vaswani et al., 2017)). Yet, these methods require large parallel corpora which are lacking for the RC content in Middle French.

Expected Outcomes The main outcome of RCnum is an open-source ergonomic and dynamic platform which will offer RC original transcriptions along with their normalised, modernised, translated and semantically enriched content, accessible through data exploration tools. For the normalisation and modernisation tasks (detailed in Figure 1), we will leverage low-resource MT techniques, e.g. fine-tuning large language models (LLMs) and artificial data generation, resulting

Proceedings of the 25th Annual Conference of the European Association for Machine Translation (Volume 2), pages 21–22
June 24-27, 2024 ©2024 European Association for Machine Translation

Manuscript

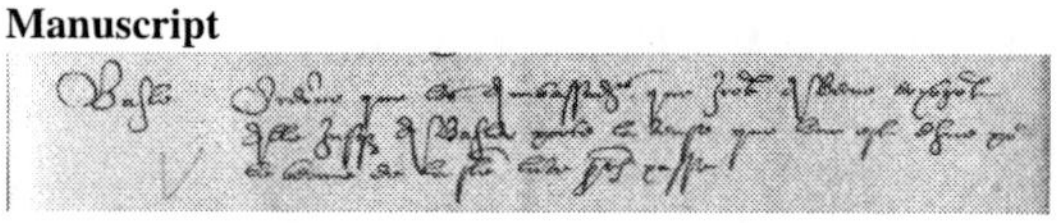

Step 1: Manual transcription
(Basle) — Ordonne que les ambassadeurs que iront a Berne doybgent alle jusque a Basle porte la cense que leur est dhue pour le terme de la saincte luce prochain passe.

Step 2: Local normalisation
(Bâle) – Ordonné que les ambassadeurs que iront à Berne doivent aller jusqu'à Bâle porter le cens que leur est dû pour le terme de la Sainte-Luce prochaine passée.

Step 3: Syntactic normalisation
(Bâle) – Il a été ordonné que les ambassadeurs qui iront à Berne doivent aller jusqu'à Bâle porter le cens qui leur est dû pour le terme de la Sainte-Lucie prochaine passée.

Step 4: Modernisation
(Bâle) – Il a été ordonné que les ambassadeurs qui iront à Berne doivent aller jusqu'à Bâle pour apporter les intérêts échus à la Sainte-Lucie passée.

Step 5: Translation
(Basel) – It has been ordered that the ambassadors who will go to Bern must go to Basel to bring the loan interests which were due on the past Saint Lucy's Day.

Figure 1: Sample taken from the Geneva Council meeting minutes held on January 5th, 1545, manually transcribed, normalised, modernised and translated.

in several versions of the corpus linked through token alignments and enriched with external information. Enrichment will be based on representation structures such as knowledge graphs combined with Linked Open Data sources (Hogan et al., 2021; Munnelly et al., 2018). The enriched corpus will contain information about named entities, dates, etc., facilitating RC modernisation with MT techniques enhanced with glossaries covering historical word forms (Dougal and Lonsdale, 2020). Simultaneously to these tasks, we will work on identifying historians and non-experts' needs in terms of user interfaces in order to design an interactive platform based on semantically enriched data visualisation techniques (Knabben et al., 2021). Furthermore, the platform will allow data enrichment through input and validation by the community. Interactive tools adapted to RC content will be evaluated with user-based tests and iterative processes aiming at improving the UI/UX (Isenberg et al., 2013).

First Results RC normalisation experiments are presented in Rubino et al. (2024b), focusing on spelling variants reduction while preserving 16th century historical wordforms. A pre-trained LLM baseline fine-tuned on a small parallel corpus outperformed previously released models trained for the normalisation of Early Modern French, as indicated by automatic metrics. Further experiments with synthetic data generation improved over this baseline. To validate these findings, we conducted a manual evaluation through post-editing, comparing normalisation from scratch to our automatic normalisation approaches (Rubino et al., 2024a).

Acknowledgements

This project is funded by the Swiss National Science Foundation (Grant n. 215733).

References

Dougal, Duane K. and Deryle Lonsdale. 2020. Improving NMT Quality Using Terminology Injection. In *LREC*, pages 4820–4827.

Hogan, Aidan, Eva Blomqvist, Michael Cochez, Claudia D'amato, Gerard De Melo, Claudio Gutierrez, Sabrina Kirrane, José Emilio Labra Gayo, Roberto Navigli, Sebastian Neumaier, Axel-Cyrille Ngonga Ngomo, Axel Polleres, Sabbir M. Rashid, Anisa Rula, Lukas Schmelzeisen, Juan Sequeda, Steffen Staab, and Antoine Zimmermann. 2021. Knowledge Graphs. *ACM Computing Surveys*, 54(4):1–37.

Isenberg, Tobias, Petra Isenberg, Jian Chen, Michael Sedlmair, and Torsten Möller. 2013. A Systematic Review on the Practice of Evaluating Visualization. *IEEE Transactions on Visualization and Computer Graphics*, 19(12):2818–2827.

Knabben, Moritz, Martin Baumann, Tanja Blascheck, Thomas Ertl, and Steffen Koch. 2021. Visualizing Temporal-Thematic Patterns in Text Collections. In *Vision, Modeling, and Visualization*, pages 9–16.

Munnelly, Gary, Harshvardhan J Pandit, and Séamus Lawless. 2018. Exploring Linked Data for the Automatic Enrichment of Historical Archives. In *The Semantic Web: ESWC*, pages 423–433.

Rubino, Raphael, Sandra Coram-Mekkey, Johanna Gerlach, Jonathan Mutal, and Pierrette Bouillon. 2024a. Automatic Normalisation of Middle French and its Impact on Productivity. In *LT4HALA*.

Rubino, Raphael, Johanna Gerlach, Jonathan David Mutal, and Pierrette Bouillon. 2024b. Normalizing without Modernizing: Keeping Historical Wordforms of Middle French while Reducing Spelling Variants. In *Findings of NAACL*.

Vaswani, Ashish, Noam Shazeer, Niki Parmar, Jakob Uszkoreit, Llion Jones, Aidan N Gomez, Ł ukasz Kaiser, and Illia Polosukhin. 2017. Attention is All you Need. In *Advances in Neural Information Processing Systems*, volume 30.

MTPE quality evaluation in translator education: the postedit.me app

Marie-Aude Lefer, Romane Bodart, Justine Piette, Adam Obrusník
UCLouvain, Louvain-la-Neuve, Belgium
marie-aude.lefer@uclouvain.be, romane.bodart@uclouvain.be,
justine@tradorizon.com, adam.obrusnik@gmail.com

Abstract

This article presents the main functionality of the postedit.me app. Postedit.me is a software program that supports machine translation post-editing training in translator education, with special emphasis on standardized quality evaluation of post-edited texts produced by students. The app is made freely available to universities for teaching and research purposes.

1 Background

Translation curricula across the globe are regularly updated to reflect the most recent technological advances in the language services industry. Machine translation post-editing (MTPE) is a case in point. While the first concrete proposals to incorporate MTPE training into translator education emerged in the 2010s, many translation curricula nowadays feature MTPE training in the form of stand-alone technology modules or language-pair-specific practical courses. Surprisingly, however, there are relatively few digital tools that support MTPE training and learning. Examples include MATEO (Vanroy et al., 2023), a web interface devoted to machine translation (MT) evaluation training, and COPECO (Mutal et al., 2020), an online collaborative platform designed to collect an annotated student post-editing corpus. In this article, we describe the postedit.me app. The tool streamlines assignment of MTPE tasks to students and automates standardized quality evaluation of students' post-edited texts.

2 Basic functionality

The postedit.me app consists of a teacher interface and a student interface. Its main objective is to help MTPE trainers assess the quality of the post-edited texts produced by their students, relying on standardized annotation taxonomies. Students are asked to carry out their MTPE assignments in dedicated computer-aided translation (CAT) tools, and to use postedit.me to submit their final post-edited texts, consult their trainer's feedback and track their progress across tasks.

2.1 MTPE task creation

MTPE tasks in postedit.me consist of three components: the source text (ST) selected by the trainer, its MT (generated by the trainer) and a set of post-editing guidelines for the task. Trainers are asked to input some metadata related to the ST (domain, genre, target readership, etc.), MT (MT tool used, glossary integration, date, etc.) and post-editing task (task conditions, timing, marking, etc.).

2.2 MT error annotation

Once a task is created, the trainer will error-annotate the MT. MT error annotation relies on the taxonomy of the Translation-oriented Annotation System (TAS) developed for translator education (Granger and Lefer, 2021), i.e., *mechanics*, *grammar and syntax*, *lexis and terminology*, *discourse and pragmatics*, *register and style*, *content*, *culture* and *brief*. MT annotation does not rely on an absolute notion of translation error. Rather, it is dependent on the pedagogical context in which the task is to be performed. In certain cases, for instance, trainers can decide to restrict their annotation to the most serious MT errors, leaving minor errors unannotated since students are not expected to edit them (e.g. because they are at an early stage of their MTPE training). The MT error annotation is only shared with students when they have completed the task and accessed their trainer's feedback.

2.3 MTPE quality evaluation

Once students have performed the MTPE task in a CAT tool, they submit their final post-edited text, together with some personal and task-related metadata, on the student interface. Students' assignments are then automatically made available on the teacher annotation interface, which features a four-column display: (1) the ST, (2) the error-annotated MT, (3) the student's raw post-edited text, and (4) the 'autocompare' version of the post-edited text and the MT, where word-level differences (additions, deletions and substitutions) are

Proceedings of the 25th Annual Conference of the European Association for Machine Translation (Volume 2), pages 23–24
June 24-27, 2024 ©2024 European Association for Machine Translation

highlighted in different colours. MTPE quality evaluation relies on the taxonomy of the Machine Translation Post-Editing Annotation System (MTPEAS; Lefer et al., 2022), which contains seven categories: *value-adding edit*, *successful edit*, *unnecessary edit*, *incomplete edit*, *error-introducing edit*, *unsuccessful edit* and *missing edit*. Missing edits are automatically identified in the tool on the basis of the prior MT error annotation performed by the trainer. The other MTPE tags are inserted by the trainer. All annotations can be augmented with comments. There is also a dedicated box for general feedback. A grade is automatically computed on the basis of the annotations, using a customizable formula (with bonuses and penalties).

2.4 MTPE quality statistics reports

Statistics reports are generated automatically, at different levels (students, individual tasks, language pairs), and are made available as raw figures and relative frequencies per 1,000 tokens, in the form of both tables and graphs. Students can access their own personal statistics on the student interface. This makes it possible to identify their main weaknesses and track their progress throughout the MTPE tasks.

2.5 Search tool

Postedit.me features automatic sentence-level alignment of ST, MT and post-edited text. On the basis of the sentence-aligned database, it is possible to query words, phrases, TAS annotations and MTPE annotations. The search tool can be used to devise data-informed tailored exercises for students and to carry out empirical research on the post-editing data collected through the app.

3 Technologies used

Postedit.me is a server application with a web interface that runs on any system supporting docker containers, primarily modern Linux. The technology stack of the app consists of several components which are all interfaced by python 3. The interface of the application is implemented in `django-framework`. The app benefits especially from the built-in Object-Relational Mapper model and the ability to easily generate forms from data models. For handling asynchronous tasks (text alignment, POS tagging), the `celery` library is used with `RabbitMQ` broker. For MT and MTPE annotation, the `LabelStudio` library is used. The app uses `SpaCy` with appropriate pre-trained models for generating POS tags and lemmas. The text alignment is quite innovative as it supports alignment of three language versions. For this reason, it mostly uses original, dedicated code, although it also calls on a few methods from `sentence_transformers` and `nltk` packages. Finally, the annotated and aligned texts are stored in a custom XML format, which is processed by the `BeautifulSoup` library. The search function is based on `ElasticSearch`, where a custom token mapping is defined, which stores a token context (N neighboring tokens) together with each token from the text. While this solution is heavy on data storage, it maximizes the speed of the concordance and supports multi-argument queries (e.g. a specific POS followed by a specific word with a specific annotation). Load-balancing is currently achieved by distributing computation-heavy tasks (alignment, POS tagging) of individual texts between computer cores.

4 App availability and licensing

The postedit.me app is made freely available to universities for teaching and internal research purposes. A custom licence agreement must be signed by both parties before the code, documentation and user guides are shared. On-demand custom commercial licences can be prepared for other partners, depending on the particular needs of interested parties (e.g. interoperability with specific CAT tools).

Acknowledgements

We gratefully acknowledge the financial support of UCLouvain's *Fonds de Développement Pédagogique* (2021–2023).

References

Granger, Sylviane, and Marie-Aude Lefer. 2021. *Translation-oriented Annotation System manual (Version 2.0). CECL Papers 3*. Louvain-la-Neuve: CECL/UCLouvain. https://uclouvain.be/en/research-institutes/ilc/cecl/cecl-papers.html

Lefer, Marie-Aude, Justine Piette, and Romane Bodart. 2022. *Machine Translation Post-Editing Annotation System (MTPEAS) manual*. OER-UCLouvain. https://oer.uclouvain.be/jspui/handle/20.500.12279/829

Mutal, Jonathan, Pierrette Bouillon, Perrine Schumacher, and Johanna Gerlach. 2020. COPECO: a Collaborative Post-Editing Corpus in Pedagogical Context. In *Proceedings of the 1st Workshop on Post-Editing in Modern-Day Translation*, 61–78, virtual.

Vanroy, Bram, Arda Tezcan, and Lieve Macken. 2023. MATEO: MAchine Translation Evaluation Online. In Mary Nurminen et al. (eds.), *Proceedings of the 24th Annual Conference of the European Association for Machine Translation*, 499–500, Tampere, Finland.

Boosting machine translation with AI-powered terminology features

Marek Sabo, Judith Klein, Giorgio Bernardinello
STAR AG
Wiesholz 35
CH-8262 Ramsen
{ marek.sabo, judith.klein, giorgio.bernardinello }
@star-group.net

Abstract

Artificial intelligence (AI) is quickly becoming an exciting new technology for the translation industry in form of large language models (LLMs). AI-based functionality could be used to improve the output of neural machine translation (NMT). One main issue that impacts MT quality and reliability is incorrect terminology. This is why STAR is making AI-powered terminology control a priority for its translation products because of the significant gains to be made — greatly improving the quality of MT output, reducing postediting (PE) costs and efforts, and thereby boosting overall translation productivity.

1 Improving terminology accuracy in MT output

The lack of correct terminology in MT output often requires extensive manual postediting to improve accuracy and consistency, which can be addressed at three stages of the translation process:

MT system selection — before translation: A customised MT model could be selected that is trained for more appropriate terminology usage compared to generic systems.

Terminology injection — during translation: More and more MT systems like DeepL or Textshuttle offer terminology support through user-provided bilingual glossaries. While compliance with the term specifications is mostly good, there are still grammatical errors when inserting terms or they do not fit with interdependent words.

Correcting terminology — after translation: The last stage for correcting terminology is on the MT output. This might be mostly necessary if (1) either no customised MT was used or did not perform correctly, (2) the system does not support terminology injection or not for the selected language, (3) the provided glossary term was not used, or it lacked morphological adaptation, or resulted in grammatical errors in other parts of the translation.

2 AI-powered terminology extraction

Numerous in-house translation projects at STAR have confirmed that terminology injection in MT output significantly reduces postediting efforts. The integration of this functionality in CAT tools, such as DeepL within STAR Transit, has become a standard practice in translation workflows, thus expanding its usage at a larger scale yielding growing benefits. With the growing demand for suitable MT glossaries, a fast and reliable terminology extraction method is crucial to boost the production of bilingual glossaries in a translation business driven by MT. This function could significantly enhance the productivity of MTPE.

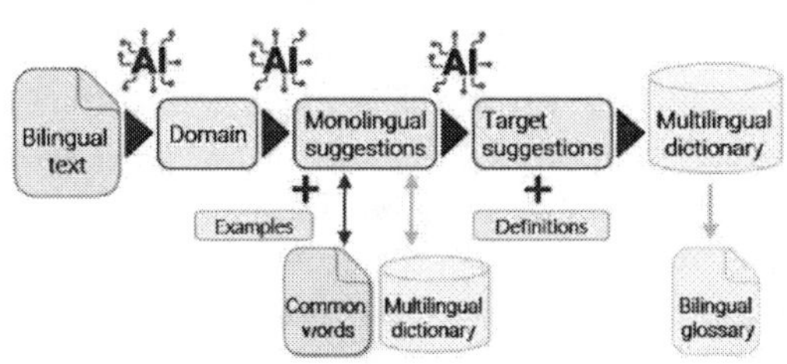

Figure 1: AI-powered bilingual terminology extraction

Powered by AI, STAR Transit in combination with TermStar (integrated terminology management tool) will deliver automatic extraction of

Proceedings of the 25th Annual Conference of the European Association for Machine Translation (Volume 2), pages 25–26
June 24-27, 2024 ©2024 European Association for Machine Translation

bilingual terminology from a translated project or a selected part of the translation memory.

With one click on the AI-powered term extraction feature a carefully-designed prompt is issued to an LLM that identifies the domain as well as candidate source language terms for that domain. These terms are checked against entries in the TermStar dictionary and a user-specific common words list. For the unmatched suggestions the corresponding target terms are extracted from the target language segment. In addition, the source segment is extracted for context, and another prompt is used to create a definition. Before being imported into the dictionary, the proposed entries are validated by human experts.

Some MT systems, e.g. Textshuttle.com, use the TermStar dictionary directly in STAR Transit for term injection while for others, like DeepL.com, the user exports the bilingual list and uploads it in STAR Transit to the MT system.

The seamless integration of the AI features in the terminology extraction function makes them both accessible and easy to use. User feedback and results will lead to improvements for various specific term extractions with additional pre-defined and customized prompts. Initial tests are being carried out with GPT-4-Turbo and GPT-3.5-Turbo for German, English, French, Italian and Spanish but further tests are also planned with smaller, local models.

3 AI-powered terminology correction in MT output

At STAR, development is underway of an AI-enhanced term correction feature, injecting terms to the MT output. As a proof of concept, we have selected English and Swedish as source languages and Slovak, a highly inflected lower-resourced European language as the target language.

We have trained a local model sized under 2 billion parameters for term injection into Slovak. The required MT glossary could be extracted from a domain-specific TermStar dictionary.

The AI term correction function scans and compares source and target text against the glossary, automatically inserting matched terms and ensuring adherence to declension patterns, gender conventions, and inflectional morphemes for each word to maintain syntactic role consistency. The feature will adjust related words like adjectives, verbs, or pronouns associated with the term, ensuring not only accuracy but also fluency in the translation, as shown in this example:

Source	Which screw terminal did you see mentioned in that manual?
DeepL	Ktorý skrutkový terminál ste videli uvedený v tejto príručke?
Terms	manual = manuál screw terminal = hlavičková svorka
Edited	Ktor~~ý~~ú ~~skrutkový~~ ~~terminál~~ hlavičkovú svorku ste videli uvede~~ný~~ú v t~~ej~~omto ~~príručke~~ manuáli?
Final	Ktorú hlavičkovú svorku ste videli uvedenú v tomto manuáli?

Table 1: Injected terms and their related words have been adjusted for case and grammar.

A major benefit of this approach is the flexibility of the solution, since the term correction can be applied to any MT output. Our current focus is on (1) finding the ideal model size to attain the best quality and speed, (2) exploring innovative approaches to dataset preparation, and (3) looking into domain matching and improvements in term alignment.

The AI-powered term correction can work with large LLMs, but the smaller models, customized for this specific task, are cost-effective, suitable for running on average laptops without GPU demands, guarantee data privacy over cloud-based LLMs, and function at stable speeds. In addition, it is easier to control their output while commercial LLMs can change at any point, affecting the dependent system.

4 Next steps

The release of the AI-powered terminology features within STAR's language technology products are scheduled for later this year. We will also investigate additional AI features for quality estimation and evaluation, with a focus on terminological accuracy, as automatic terminology correction may have failed or lead to other translation errors. In addition, we will explore the possibility of using AI to generate an image based on the term, its definition and the context-related example that supports the user's understanding of the term and its postediting.

Automatic detection of (potential) factors in the source text leading to gender bias in machine translation

Janiça Hackenbuchner **Arda Tezcan** **Joke Daems**
Language and Translation Technology Team
Department of Translation, Interpreting and Communication
Ghent University
Belgium
firstname.surname@ugent.be

Abstract

This research project aims to develop a comprehensive methodology to help make machine translation (MT) systems more gender-inclusive for society. The goal is the creation of a detection system, a machine learning (ML) model trained on manual annotations, that can automatically analyse source data and detect and highlight words and phrases that influence the gender bias inflection in target translations. The main research outputs will be (1) a manually annotated dataset, (2) a taxonomy, and (3) a fine-tuned model.

1 Credits

This project is a strategic basic PhD research fully funded by The Research Foundation – Flanders (FWO) for the timespan of four years from 01.11.2023 until 31.10.2027, and hosted within the Language and Translation Technology Team (LT3) at Ghent University.

2 Introduction

With an increasing use of and interest in the developments of machine translation (MT) and a growing demand for gender inclusiveness in society, research on gender bias in MT is increasing (Savoldi et al., 2021). An MT system is considered to be gender-biased if it "systematically and unfairly discriminates against certain individuals or groups in favor of others" (Savoldi et al., 2021, p. 846), perpetuating "inaccurate and potentially discriminatory stereotypes" in society (Vanmassenhove, 2024, p. 3).

Word-level studies show that word embeddings used in MT training are highly gender-inflected, where word embeddings of different parts-of-speech (POS) strongly cluster based on their gender in varying domains (e.g., in sports, kitchen, big tech, sexual profanities) (Caliskan et al., 2022). However, research on word embeddings is limited to word-level analysis and has not yet been extended to the full context of natural language source sentences and resulting systematic gender associations in machine translations.

3 Project Description

In this research project, we apply a novel approach to analyse aligned linguistic and morphological features with a focus on gender in source and target texts and apply machine learning methodologies.

English is chosen as the source language, where role names are generally not marked with a gender (e.g. *teacher*) and the target translations are analysed in German and Spanish, grammatical gender languages (Savoldi et al., 2021), where gender is clearly marked (e.g. *Lehrer/Lehrerin*). The aim is to automatically identify and classify "trigger words" in a source context that influence the grammatical gender inflection in the target translation (i.e. whether an MT translates a person as female or male, or instead opts to neutralise or rephrase the word). The project consists of the following main deliverables that differ from previous research: (1) a manually annotated dataset of human gender associations in sentence contexts, (2) a taxonomy based on these annotations, (3) a comparative analysis of human gender associations vs. the MT gender inflections, and (4) a fine-tuned large language model (LLM) that highlights trigger words for gender in a source text.

Proceedings of the 25th Annual Conference of the European Association for Machine Translation (Volume 2), pages 27–28
June 24-27, 2024 ©2024 European Association for Machine Translation

3.1 Data collection

The first step is the collection of a list of candidate words (role names, e.g. *friend*) including their gender inflection, as sampled from their word embeddings in previous studies. These words are used to filter monolingual English data from different domains, slightly resembling the methodology taken by Ondoño-Soler and Forcada (2022). Following the automatic filtering, the English sentences are filtered manually on a monolingual-level to select gender-ambiguous cases in terms of the singular candidate word. We aim for 2,000 to 5,000 sentences for model fine-tuning.

Next, the filtered data will be machine translated into German and Spanish with publicly available MT toolkits. We document and compare into which gender the MT systems translate each candidate word, first on a word level (e.g. the individual term *friend*) and then in a sentence context (e.g. *After a friend suggested she try it, Ann said, "Sure!"*). The two bilingual corpora (EN-DE, EN-ES) will be aligned and enriched at word level for morphosyntactic information.

3.2 Data Annotation and Analysis

In the next step, the ambiguous English data will be manually annotated to analyse how context influences gender associations. From these annotations, we can compare to what extent human gender associations overlap with an MT system's choice of grammatical gender in a target language.

For each sentence, annotators will be asked to annotate what context influences their gender association. Specifically, they are asked to annotate any trigger words or phrases (e.g., a reference, location or any POS) that they personally consider to influence the gender inflection of a candidate word in that sentence. The annotations will be verified and classified and from this, a taxonomy will be created. A case study with 22 annotators of different genders was already conducted to assess annotation guidelines, annotator agreement and gender influence (Hackenbuchner et al., under review).

Next, we will analyse morphosyntactic features of the data using automated tools. The combination of all morphosyntactic information will reveal patterns between trigger words and the candidate word in question. Based on this analysis, we want to exclude "irrelevant" trigger words, allowing us to focus on "relevant" words or phrases that have the greatest influence on the candidate's gender.

3.3 Model Fine-Tuning and Evaluation

In our final step we apply machine learning (ML) by fine-tuning an LLM based on our annotated and verified data and the information extracted from the morphosyntactic analysis. By seeking previously unstudied patterns that lead to gender bias in MT, with this fine-tuned model we aim to automatically detect gender-triggering words or phrases in a source text and highlight these.

4 Aligned Projects

In line with this research project, the PhD fellow, first author of this paper, is a co-founder and member of DeBiasByUs[1] and a co-organiser of the two International Workshops on Gender-Inclusive Translation Technologies.

5 Conclusion

Our benchmark could make MT users aware of gender inflections of source texts that are machine translated, technologically support translators in post-editing MT output, direct developers of MT systems to persisting issues of gender bias, and help content creators identify potential triggers in text that may lead to gender-biased translations.

References

Caliskan, Aylin, Pimparkar P. Ajay, Tessa Charlesworth, Robert Wolfe, and Mahzarin R. Banaji. 2022. Gender bias in word embeddings: A comprehensive analysis of frequency, syntax, and semantics. In *Proceedings of the 2022 AAAI/ACM Conference on AI, Ethics, and Society*, page 156–170.

Hackenbuchner, Janiça, Arda Tezcan, Aaron Maladry, and Joke Daems. under review. You shall know a word's gender by the company it keeps: Comparing the role of context in human gender assumptions with mt.

Ondoño-Soler, Nerea and Mikel L. Forcada. 2022. The exacerbation of (grammatical) gender stereotypes in english–spanish machine translation. *Revista Tradumàtica*, 20:177–196.

Savoldi, Beatrice, Marco Gaido, Luisa Bentivogli, Matteo Negri, and Marco Turchi. 2021. Gender bias in machine translation. In *Transactions of the Association for Computational Linguistics*, volume 9, page 845–874, Cambridge, MA.

Vanmassenhove, Eva. 2024. Gender bias in machine translation and the era of large language models. In *arXiv preprint*, page 1–24.

[1] `https://debiasbyus.ugent.be/`

INCREC: Uncovering the creative process of translated content using machine translation

Ana Guerberof Arenas
Computational Linguistics Group
University of Groningen
a.guerberof.arenas@rug.nl

Abstract

The INCREC project aims to uncover professional translators' creative stages to understand how technology can be best applied to the translation of literary and audio-visual texts, and to analyse the impact of these processes on readers and viewers. To better understand this process, INCREC triangulates data from eye-tracking, retrospective think-aloud interviews, translated material, and questionnaires from professional translators and users.

1 Introduction

A remarkably high percentage of what we read and view is translated, especially in our multilingual and global society. For this translated content to reach world-wide audiences faster and at low cost, publishers and platforms are using MT. In view of the increasing amount of interlingual communication mediated by technology that we, as a society, are exposed to, understanding its effects on translators and the resulting user experience has become a matter of urgency.

My recent research on creativity in the translated product, as part of the EU-funded project CREAMT, shows that literary texts translated with MT have a lower creativity index than those processed in a traditional way and, therefore, the user experience might be negatively impacted by MT (Guerberof-Arenas and Toral, 2020). Yet, little is known of how technology affects the creative process of professional translators, rather than the final product, or how MT could be administered to favour the translating process and, hence, the user experience. [1]

2 Previous work

In psychology, there is some agreement about the definition of creativity itself, as something that drives novel and useful ideas (Runco and Jaeger, 2012), but when it comes to the creative processes there is less agreement (Jankowska et al., 2018). Further, there is not a single model that can describe the creative process in all disciplines (Botella and Lubart, 2016). And although more empirical research has been devoted to translation processes and translation cognition in recent years (Vanroy, Schaeffer, and Macken, 2021), creativity in translation is mainly analysed from a product perspective (Bayer-Hohenwarter, 2011), or as a trait that might result in better translations (Rojo and Meseguer, 2018). A welcome change of focus, from product to process, was carried out by Kussmaul (1995). Based on the four-stage model defined by Wallas (1926), and on empirical research using think aloud protocols with translation students, he suggests a four-phase model: preparation, incubation, illumination, and evaluation. However, the process of professional translators, especially those that work within the creative industries, when technology is applied, continues to be under-researched.

3 Methodology

INCREC looks at the macro processes (stages of creativity) and micro processes (translation problems, i.e. units of creative potential, UCP) in the MT-aided translation of creative content. A research team of six (PI, three PhD students, one post-doctoral researcher and one research assistant) will implement INCREC's four work packages.

3.1 WP1 - Macro-process: stages of the creative process (3 PhDs)

WP1 involves the collection of data from forty professional literary and audiovisual (AV) translators. They will carry out a two-week long

Proceedings of the 25th Annual Conference of the European Association for Machine Translation (Volume 2), pages 29–30
June 24-27, 2024 ©2024 European Association for Machine Translation

preparatory task while taking notes on their creative process. They will be interviewed afterwards to gain insight on a) how they define creativity, b) how their creative process takes place, c) how they name the creative stages, and d) what conditions foster creativity.

3.2 WP2 - Micro-process: units of creative potential (2 PhDs)

The WP is divided into two subprojects: WP2.1 will collect data from twenty professionals translating a short story while WP2.2 will collect data from twenty professionals subtitling three related videos using an eye-tracker. The professionals will translate on their own or they will receive MT assistance either by default or on demand. A video of their gaze will be presented to obtain retrospective data. The target texts will be annotated for creative shifts (CSs) and errors. The analysis of the stages from WP1 will be contrasted with these results, and the eye-tracking data at word level will provide information on how translators deal with UCPs in a source sentence.

3.3 WP3 - Readers' preferences and attention in literary translation (PhD 3)

Fifty participants will read three extracts of literary texts using an eye-tracker. These three extracts will be randomly presented to the participants in pairs, so they can compare several modalities once (e.g. MT vs PE). The participant will thereby see two different modalities each time for the same source text and select the one they prefer. They will be prompted to explain the reasons behind their choice. Upon completion, a video of their gaze will be presented so they can describe what they were thinking or feeling when looking at certain words.

3.4 Viewers' engagement and attention in AVT translation (Post-Doc 1)

Ninety participants will watch selected movies from WP2.2, translated in different modalities using an eye-tracker. After watching the clips, the participants will then fill in a survey (Guerberof-Arenas and Toral, 2020). For AVT, we will consider mean fixation, dwell time, number of fixations, percentage of skipped subtitles and deflections to image in the different modalities.

4 Expected outcomes

The project has seven objectives: 1) Create a framework of creative stages in literary and AV translation, 2) Describe and systematically classify micro-process in literary and AV translation, 3) Understand the benefits or constraints of MT when provided at different stages to translators, 4) Understand how productivity and creativity are related in AV translation, 5) Analyse and classify user preferences in literary translation, 6) Analyse and classify how users relate to CSs in translation, 7) Analyse the role of raw MT in the reception of literary text/subtitles produced without professional intervention.

Acknowledgment

This project has received funding from the European Union's Horizon Europe research and innovation programme under ERC Consolidator Grant No. 101086819.

References

Bayer-Hohenwarter, Gerrit. 2011. Creative Shifts as a Means of Measuring and Promoting Translational Creativity, *Meta* 56 (3), 663–692.

Botella, Marion, and Todd Lubart. 2016. Creative Processes: Art, Design and Science. In *Multidisciplinary Contributions to the Science of Creative Thinking*, 53–65, Creativity in the Twenty First Century, Springer, Singapore.

Guerberof-Arenas, Ana, and Antonio Toral. 2020. The Impact of Post-Editing and Machine Translation on Creativity and Reading Experience. *Translation Spaces* 9 (2), 255–282.

Guerberof-Arenas, Ana, and Antonio Toral. 2022. Creativity in Translation: Machine Translation as a Constraint for Literary Texts. *Translation Spaces* 11 (2), 184–212.

Jankowska, Dorota M., Marta Czerwonka, Izabela Lebuda, and Maciej Karwowski. 2018. Exploring the Creative Process: Integrating Psychometric and Eye-Tracking Approaches. *Frontiers in Psychology* 9.

Kussmaul, Paul. 1995. "Creativity in Translation." *Training the Translator*, edited by Paul Kussmaul, 39–34. Benjamins Translation Library 10, John Benjamins Publishing Company, Amsterdam.

Rojo, Ana, and Purificación Meseguer. 2018. Creativity and Translation Quality: Opposing Enemies or Friendly Allies? *HERMES - Journal of Language and Communication in Business*, no. 57 (June), 79.

Runco, Mark A., and Jarret J. Jaeger. 2012. The Standard Definition of Creativity. *Creativity Research Journal* 24 (1), 92–96.

Vanroy, Bram, Moritz Schaeffer, and Lieve Macken. 2021. Comparing the Effect of Product-Based Metrics on the Translation Process. *Frontiers in Psychology* 12, 1–16

Wallas, Graham. 1926. *The Art of Thought*. Harcourt Brace and Company, New York

SMUGRI-MT - Machine Translation System for Low-Resource Finno-Ugric Languages

Taido Purason* **Aleksei Ivanov*** **Lisa Yankovskaya** **Mark Fishel**
Institute of Computer Science
University of Tartu, Estonia
{taido.purason,aleksei.ivanov,lisa.yankovskaya,mark.fisel}@ut.ee

Abstract

SMUGRI is a research project supported by an Estonian Research Council grant, aiming to develop natural language processing tools for Finno-Ugric languages and varieties. In this paper, we describe SMUGRI-MT, the part of the project that focuses on developing neural machine translation for this language family. Currently 20 low-resource Finno-Ugric languages are covered, along with seven high-resource languages.

1 Introduction

This project focuses on neural machine translation (MT) for the Finno-Ugric languages. Besides three mid-resource languages (Estonian, Finnish and Hungarian), this family includes dozens more that range from low-resource (e.g. Komi, Veps) to extremely endangered and under-supported languages (e.g. Livonian, Votic). Our goal is to include as many of these languages and varieties as possible and provide them with reliable MT models and methodology.

Our work on developing MT systems for low-resource Finno-Ugric languages started in 2021, initially focusing on Võro as well as Southern and Northern Sami (Tars et al., 2021). One year later, we added Inari, Skolt and Lule Sami languages (Tars et al., 2022) and developed an MT system for Livonian (Rikters et al., 2022). Last year, we significantly expanded the scope of our MT system to include a total of 20 low-resource languages and dialects (Yankovskaya et al., 2023). Since the last version, we have collected more data, transitioned to a different multilingual pretrained model (NLLB Team et al., 2022, 1.2B parameters, distilled) and implemented language identification and hallucination detection tests to ensure a cleaner dataset.

Below we describe the current state of the developed MT system and outline the future challenges.

2 The current stage

The version currently available online[1] is tailored for 20 low-resource languages: Mansi, Khanty, Komi, Komi-Permyak, Udmurt, Meadow and Hill Mari, North Sami, South Sami, Inari Sami, Lule Sami, Skolt Sami, Erzya, Moksha, Ludian, Proper Karelian, Võro, Veps, Livvi Karelian, Livonian along with seven high-resource languages: English, Estonian, Finnish, Hungarian, Latvian, Norwegian (Bokmål), and Russian.

Benchmark test sets are currently available for only nine low-resource languages: Komi, Udmurt, Hill and Meadow Mari, Erzya, Moksha, Livonian, Mansi, and Livvi Karelian (Yankovskaya et al., 2023). Table 1 presents the average chrF++ (Popović, 2017) and BLEU (Papineni et al., 2002) scores for these languages along with scores for seven high-resource languages presented in our MT system. In comparison with our previous MT system, the current system shows better performance, with improvements of 5-7 points in terms of chrF++ score. Translations from low-resource to high-resource languages achieved the highest performance. In contrast, translations into low-resource languages, whether from other low-resource languages or high-resource languages,

*Equal contribution

[1] https://translate.ut.ee/

Proceedings of the 25th Annual Conference of the European Association for Machine Translation (Volume 2), pages 31–32
June 24-27, 2024 ©2024 European Association for Machine Translation

demonstrated notably lower performance.

	chrF++	BLEU
low-low	32.4 (+5.2)	6.1
low-high	43.8 (+7.2)	16.8
high-low	33.9 (+7.1)	6.7

Table 1: Average chrF++ (Popović, 2017) and BLEU (Papineni et al., 2002) scores across different language pair clusters; numbers in brackets indicate the improvement of the current system over the preivous one. Low-low - translations from low-resource to low-resource, low-high - from low-resource to high-resource, high-low - from high-resource to low-resource languages.

3 Future challenges

Although this work started in 2021, the project SMUGRI-MT has received funding only recently, thus there is still a lot of work to be done more systematically. Our efforts will focus on three directions of future research:

Data: We will continue to collect parallel and monolingual data for currently supported languages, as well as expand our dataset to include new languages and varieties. In addition to data collection, we will prioritize preprocessing steps to produce cleaner corpora.

Several Finno-Ugric languages (already included and these to be added) do not have a normalized orthography and additionally represent a mixture of dialects and varieties. Therefore an important future direction is separating the varieties from each other and deciding what to do about orthographic variation.

Analysis: We plan to conduct a detailed qualitative analysis of the translations to identify errors overlooked by automatic metrics. Additionally, we aim to develop test sets across various domains and language varieties, enabling a more comprehensive qualitative and quantitative analysis.

Architecture: The current system translates one sentence at a time. We have plans to transition to paragraph-level and document-level systems to reduce at least gender-related issues. This is mainly due to the Finno-Ugric languages being gender-neutral, making it impossible to determine the correct gender without context and making it important to translate genders consistently throughout the document when generating a language with grammatical gender (like English).

Acknowledgments

This work was partially supported by the Estonian Research Council grant PRG2006 as well as the National Programme of Estonian Language Technology grant EKTB67. All computations were performed on the LUMI Supercomputer through the University of Tartu's HPC center.

References

NLLB Team, Marta R. Costa-jussà, James Cross, Onur Çelebi, Maha Elbayad, Kenneth Heafield, Kevin Heffernan, Elahe Kalbassi, Janice Lam, Daniel Licht, Jean Maillard, Anna Sun, Skyler Wang, Guillaume Wenzek, Al Youngblood, Bapi Akula, Loic Barrault, Gabriel Mejia-Gonzalez, Prangthip Hansanti, John Hoffman, Semarley Jarrett, Kaushik Ram Sadagopan, Dirk Rowe, Shannon Spruit, Chau Tran, Pierre Andrews, Necip Fazil Ayan, Shruti Bhosale, Sergey Edunov, Angela Fan, Cynthia Gao, Vedanuj Goswami, Francisco Guzmán, Philipp Koehn, Alexandre Mourachko, Christophe Ropers, Safiyyah Saleem, Holger Schwenk, and Jeff Wang. 2022. No language left behind: Scaling human-centered machine translation. *arXiv preprint arXiv:2207.04672*.

Papineni, Kishore, Salim Roukos, Todd Ward, and Wei-Jing Zhu. 2002. Bleu: a method for automatic evaluation of machine translation. In *Proceedings of the 40th Annual Meeting of the Association for Computational Linguistics*, pages 311–318.

Popović, Maja. 2017. chrF++: words helping character n-grams. In *Proceedings of the Second Conference on Machine Translation (WMT'17)*, pages 612–618.

Rikters, Matīss, Marili Tomingas, Tuuli Tuisk, Valts Ernštreits, and Mark Fishel. 2022. Machine translation for Livonian: Catering to 20 speakers. In *Proceedings of the 60th Annual Meeting of the Association for Computational Linguistics (Volume 2: Short Papers)*, pages 508–514.

Tars, Maali, Andre Tättar, and Mark Fišel. 2021. Extremely low-resource machine translation for closely related languages. In *Proceedings of the 23rd Nordic Conference on Computational Linguistics (NoDaLiDa)*, pages 41–52.

Tars, Maali, Andre Tättar, and Mark Fišel. 2022. Cross-lingual transfer from large multilingual translation models to unseen under-resourced languages. *Baltic Journal of Modern Computing*, 10.3:435–446.

Yankovskaya, Lisa, Maali Tars, Andre Tättar, and Mark Fishel. 2023. Machine translation for low-resource Finno-Ugric languages. In *Proceedings of the 24th Nordic Conference on Computational Linguistics (NoDaLiDa)*, pages 762–771.

plain X: 4-in-1 multilingual adaptation platform

Peggy van der Kreeft & Mirko Lorenz
Deutsche Welle, Bonn, Germany
peggy.van-der-kreeft@dw.com
mirko.lorenz@dw.com

Carlos Amaral
Priberam, Lisbon, Portugal
carlos@priberam.pt

Abstract

plain X is a 4-in-1 solution for language adaptation. The software is an outcome of European HLT research and is by now in use as the major artificial-intelligence-powered human language processing platform at Deutsche Welle. plain X is a one-stop-shop for automated transcription, translation, subtitling and voice-over, with human correction options at all stages. We demonstrate how the platform works and show new features and developments of the platform in the framework of the SELMA project.[1]

1 Introduction

plain X is a 4-in-1 software enabling the use of multiple AI language engines and feature-driven workflows for transcription, translation, subtitling and (synthetic) voice-over.

The platform is an outcome of European Research projects and is a joint development by the Portuguese SME Priberam and the German public world broadcaster Deutsche Welle (DW).

2 Current Use

plain X is currently live in DW, so used in production, and being rolled out further in the organization to enable thousands of editors to work with the platform. At present, some 1000 are registered. It is used to subtitle news items and documentaries in the source language, as well as to create adaptations into the 32 languages currently covered by DW. The objective for DW is to have a system in place that enables it to subtitle all its newly published content by the end of 2025.

Since late 2022, the platform is available to any organization, as a software-as-a-service offering. It is in active use by some media and content clients and in test phase by more. Not only the media sector is targeted, but potentially any organization, large or small, dealing with content that needs subtitling or adaptation.

Ongoing efforts involve integration of the platform in the clients' infrastructures, ensuring the different systems are linked and exchanging information and data.

3 plain X Basics

A few concepts are key to the platform.

It has been co-developed by Deutsche Welle and user requirements are very much at the heart of the platform. User feedback and demands over the past two years helped to simplify the workflow and to increase productivity.

plain X serves as a one-stop shop. It provides a single, user-friendly, tool for four major functions, i.e., transcription, translation, subtitling and voice-over. Instead of juggling between different tools, the user can do all that in one and the same platform. For many users it is the first encounter with new AI engines as part of their daily work.

The platform works as a gateway to different service providers, such as Google Translate, DeepL, eTranslation or GoURMET[2] MT tools. This also allows us to keep up to date on new developments and add new engines and services in a fairly short timeframe. The platform can connect to any language engine with an API. This flexibility is very important, as new developments and even entirely new AI content tools come to the market. Being able to add new

[1] https://selma-project.eu
[2] https://gourmet-project.eu/

Proceedings of the 25th Annual Conference of the European Association for Machine Translation (Volume 2), pages 33–34
June 24-27, 2024 ©2024 European Association for Machine Translation

engines when they become available is needed to not fall behind with the entire platform. At present, the platform integrates 10 MT service providers, covering 177 unique target languages, obviously resulting in a high number of language pairs. This aggregation approach takes us far from the traditional one-engine service and allows us to connect to a variety of engines. plain X acts as a hub for new engines. It is a sign of the times: plain X is both a result of and an answer to the issue of engines. Users should be guided to the best possible solution for each language pair, including low-resourced languages.

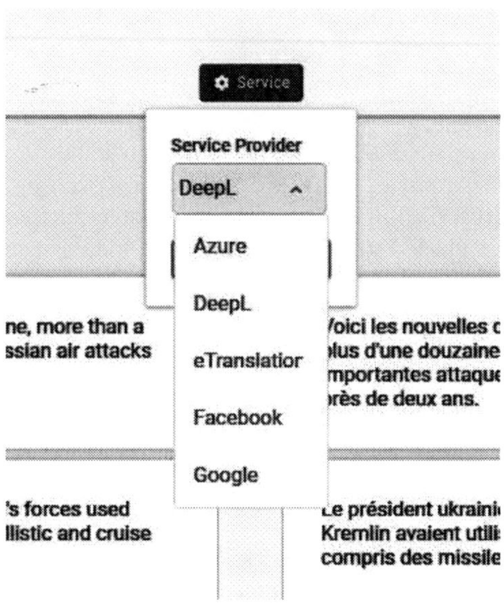

Figure 1: Translation mode with choice of engines in plain X

Deciding which engine is best for a given language pair is one of the major current challenges. Recently, DW has developed a user-friendly benchmarking system, incorporating both automated evaluation, using BLEU and chrF scores as well as TER (Translation Error Rate) for MT, and human rating. This enables us to involve native speakers and do a fast assessment in case of new or updated engines or to identify low-quality output for certain language pairs.

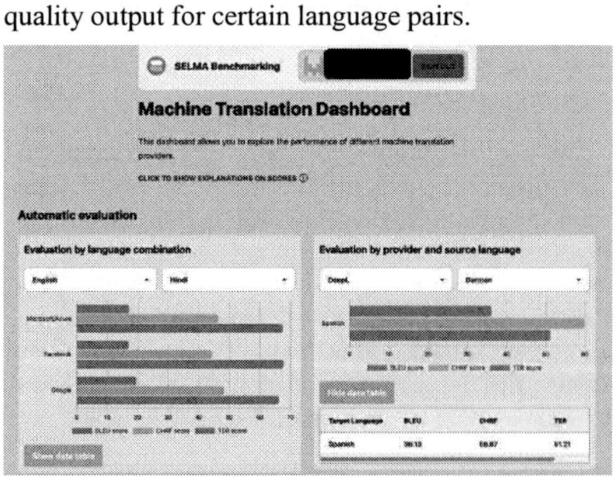

Figure 2: DW MT Benchmarking System

The platform is very goal oriented. For example: The user can instruct the platform to create English subtitles for a report in English, without having to go through every step manually. plain X would first transcribe, then translate and finally create the subtitles.

A key concept of plain X is to support the human in the loop. Users can intervene at all stages of the process. This is particularly important in the translation phase, as post-editing is definitely required before publication. In the end, the editor remains responsible for the quality of published content. We are aiming at efficiency, increased productivity, with accuracy at the center, yet without over-editing.

4 Enhanced Features

We will outline some major recent enhancements to the platform and the use of plain X.

We have added speaker diarization, resulting in adding speaker labels to a transcription and subsequent translation, subtitle or voice-over, which is particularly important in case of interviews or discussions.

Various export formats have been added for translation as well as subtitling output, following user demand. Customization and enhancement of subtitling templates allows users to set the subtitle style and font adapted to their language and brand, and ensuring that subtitles are not covering inserts, as is too often still the case.

Accessibility is also high on the agenda and the latest version takes into account aspects such as contrast colors, key shortcuts (reducing the need to work with the mouse), descriptive text for images and functions, etc.

The platform supports collaborative work and tasks can be assigned to teams as well as individuals, ensuring work can easily be shared with colleagues, vital in a time-critical multilingual news production environment. In particular for translations, the four-eyes principle is applied for adequate quality control.

Acknowledgments

This work has received funding from the European Union's Horizon 2020 research and innovation program under grant agreement No 957017, Project SELMA.

The BridgeAI Project

Helena Moniz
University of Lisbon/INESC-ID
helena.moniz@campus.ul.pt

Joana Lamego
Champalimaud Foundation
joana.lamego@research.fchampalimaud.org

Nuno André, António Novais, Bruno Prezado Silva, Maria Ana Henriques, Mariana Dalblon, Paulo Dimas, Pedro Vale Gonçalves
Unbabel
{nuno.andre, antonio.novais, bruno, maria.henriques, mariana.dalblon.int, pdimas, pedro.goncalves}@unbabel.com

Abstract

This paper describes the project "BridgeAI: Boosting Regulatory Implementation with Data-driven insights, Global expertise, and Ethics for AI", a one-year science-for-policy research project funded by the Portuguese Foundation for Science and Technology (FCT). The project aims to provide decision-makers in Portugal with the best context to implement the EU Artificial Intelligence (AI) Act and bridge the gap between AI research and policy. Although not exclusively on machine translation, the project pertains to natural language processing in general and ultimately to each of us as citizens.

1 Introduction

World-leading researchers in artificial intelligence (AI) hold differing views on the potential risks of AI in the future and on the need and intensity of AI regulation (Novelli et al., 2023). These divergent views reinforce the need to align regulation and implementation with scientific evidence, informing decision-makers about real risks, opportunities, and future pathways.

Historically, the outcomes from science –policy interfaces have not proved to be straightforward and do not usually lead to the establishment of effective collaborations (Jagannathan et al., 2023). The process by which knowledge is transferred from scientists to decision-makers is usually considered ineffective, due to a lack of understanding.

Furthermore, the recent approval of the EU AI Act (AIA) by the European Parliament mandates swift implementation by Member States, presenting numerous societal and scientific challenges.

BridgeAI aims to respond to these challenges, by moving towards a context-based approach that facilitates the creation of actionable knowledge at the intersection of science and practical, ethical, social, legal, and political domains. BridgeAI's primary objective is to furnish decision-makers and relevant stakeholders with comprehensive contextual insights through the analysis of real-world case studies, and the collaboration between AI experts and decision-makers. By doing so, we aim to enhance the informed and effective implementation of the AIA in Portugal and empower stakeholders to transition from passive compliance with regulations to active participation in the responsible design of AI internationally (Floridi et al, 2018).

2 Project overview

BridgeAI's proposal for the science-for-policy project received approval in March 2024. Scheduled to initiate in April, the project entails six months of preparatory work followed by a three-day workshop in Lisbon. This workshop will convene experts from diverse fields organised into different working groups (WGs) to formulate recommendations for the application of the AIA by the Portuguese Public Administration. The concluding day of the workshop will feature presentations of findings and a roundtable discussion on broader topics, open to the public.

Subsequent to the workshop, a detailed analysis of discussions and recommendations will be conducted, culminating in the formulation of a positional paper to aid the Portuguese public administration in crafting a coherent strategy for the implementation of the AIA. The project is designed to impact beyond 2024, and should include broader activities topics such as AI literacy to the public domain.

Proceedings of the 25th Annual Conference of the European Association for Machine Translation (Volume 2), pages 35–36
June 24-27, 2024 ©2024 European Association for Machine Translation

2.1 Key partners and people

Currently, BridgeAI counts with the following partners: Anacom, British Embassy Lisbon, Champalimaud Foundation, INESC-ID, Instituto de Telecomunicações, JLM&A, SGS, The Alan Turing Institute, Unbabel, and VdA. The team is investing a significant effort into engaging with more partners from the public administration.

2.2 Methodology

During the six-month preparatory work, distinct working groups (WG) will lay the groundwork for the workshop. Each WG, comprising approximately seven members, will focus on specific areas:

WG0 | AI technological case studies: Foundational and transversal WG that will create the case studies of AI products from the Center for responsible AI, serving as the basis for other WGs.

WG1 | Risk Assessment tools in AI products: Determine what should be in a practical AI risk assessment tool for public and private entities, based on tools already available to assess responsible AI principles (Morley et al., 2019).

WG2 | AI Ethics in Regulatory Processes: Taking into consideration the case-studies, the WG will define how we should address AI ethical concerns in the regulatory processes and how to provide ethical training at several levels.

WG3 | AI Act interface with other regulations, norms, audits and implementation metrics: Determine the key implementation initiatives that should arise to ensure the AI Act is effectively implemented and that all are conciliated (*e.g.*, certification, standards, audits and control).

WG4 | Advanced training and literacy: Define strategic measures for Portugal to increase levels of AI literacy and propose training programs to be developed. Based on actionable knowledge (Stern et al., 2020) methodologies and a diverse team, this WG will work to make responsible AI explicit to the public administration and citizens.

WG5 | AI ethics and regulatory efforts outside the EU: Point out best practices in AI regulation and ethics being developed outside the EU and understand how Portugal can learn from these or align best practices across legal frameworks.

To ensure the workshop is productive and insightful, preparatory work will feature periodic meetings and progress reports. Each WG will determine topics to be discussed in the workshop, and all members should be informed and aware of state-of-the-art scientific insights. Each WG will be led by a coordinator responsible for facilitating group efforts. Following the workshop, the project management team will distil the accumulated actionable knowledge to produce the expected outcomes and outreach to the core stakeholders.

2.3 Expected outcomes

The anticipated outcomes of the project encompass a positional paper to be submitted to the public administration, comprising well-founded, concrete, and actionable recommendations for the AIA implementation in Portugal, and an additional list of recommendations outlining a medium to long-term plan for the successful implementation of the AIA by the public administration, preparing the economy to the new paradigm of AI.

3 Acknowledgements

This project is funded by the Portuguese Science Foundation (FCT), under the science-for-policy programme, thematic area "Antecipar a regulação da Inteligência Artificial" reference 2023.10424.S4P23.

References

Floridi, L., Cowls, J., Beltrametti, M., Chatila, R., Chazerand, P., Dignum, V., Luetge, C., Madelin, R., Pagallo, U., Rossi, F., Schäfer, B., Valcke, P., & Vayena, E. 2018. AI4People—An Ethical Framework for a Good AI Society: Opportunities, Risks, Principles, and Recommendations. *Minds and Machines*, 28(4), 689–707.

Jagannathan, K., Emmanuel, G., Arnott, J., Mach, K. J., Bamzai-Dodson, A., Goodrich, K., Meyer, R., Neff, M., Sjostrom, K. D., Timm, K. M., Turnhout, E., Wong-Parodi, G., Bednarek, A. T., Meadow, A., Dewulf, A., Kirchhoff, C. J., Moss, R. H., Nichols, L., Oldach, E., … Klenk, N. 2023. A research agenda for the science of actionable knowledge: Drawing from a review of the most misguided to the most enlightened claims in the science-policy interface literature. *Environmental Science & Policy*, 144, 174–186..

Moniz, H. & Escartín, C. 2023. Towards Responsible Machine Translation: Ethical and Legal Considerations in Machine Translation. Springer, *Machine Translation: Technologies and Applications*, 4.

Morley, J., Floridi, L., Kinsey, L., and Elhalal, A. 2019. From What to How: An Initial Review of Publicly Available AI Ethics Tools, Methods and Research to Translate Principles into Practices. *Science and Engineering Ethics*, 26(4), 2141–2168.

Novelli, C. C., Casolari, F., Rotolo, A., Taddeo, M. & Floridi, L. 2023. Taking AI risks seriously: a new assessment model for the AI Act. *AI & SOCIETY*.

Stern, M. J., Briske, D. D., & Meadow, A. M. 2021. Opening learning spaces to create actionable knowledge for conservation. *Conservation Science and Practice*, 3(5), e378.

GeFMT: Gender-Fair Language in German Machine Translation

Manuel Lardelli
University of Graz / Austria
manuel.lardelli@uni-graz.at

Anne Lauscher
University of Hamburg / Germany
anne.lauscher@uni-hamburg.de

Giuseppe Attanasio
Instituto de Telecomunicações / Lisbon, Portugal
giuseppeattanasio6@gmail.com

Abstract

Research on gender bias in Machine Translation (MT) predominantly focuses on binary gender or few languages. In this project, we investigate the ability of commercial MT systems and neural models to translate using gender-fair language (GFL) from English into German. We enrich a community-created GFL dictionary, and sample multi-sentence test instances from encyclopedic text and parliamentary speeches. We translate our resources with different MT systems and open-weights models. We also plan to post-edit biased outputs with professionals and share them publicly. The outcome will constitute a new resource for automatic evaluation and modeling gender-fair EN-DE MT.

1 Background

A wealth of research in the field of Machine Translation (MT) focuses on gender bias (Savoldi et al., 2021). However, most recent efforts predominantly focus on binary gender only (Lardelli and Gromann, 2023) or few languages. For instance, first contributions benchmark gender-neutral language in English-to-Italian MT (Piergentili et al., 2023). Gender-neutrality refers to avoiding gender-specific elements, often by rewording sentences with indefinite pronouns and passive constructions, amongst others. In contrast to gender-neutrality, new proposals advocate for gender-inclusive translation, e.g., by accounting for neopronouns (e.g., *xe/xem*), neomorphemes and characters such as the gender star (*) in German (e.g., *der*die Berater*in*). Such approaches increase gender visibility and might therefore be preferred for reference to non-binary individuals.

2 Project Overview

The present project is a one-year joint effort of the University of Graz and Hamburg, and the Instituto de Telecomunicações in Lisbon. It encompasses (*i*) the creation of a dataset we will share with the community for gender-fair MT,[1] (*ii*) human and automatic assessment of the use (or lack thereof) of gender-fair language in different commercial and non-commercial MT systems, and (*iii*) test new methods to generate translations based on gender-fair post-edited datasets. These steps are detailed in the following paragraphs.

(*i*) We use a community-generated gender-fair dictionary in German as a basis for our experiments.[2] This dictionary lists numerous common nouns and gender-neutral alternatives proposed by people who engage in language inclusivity. Drawing on this resource, we create a dataset by randomly selecting 128 entries and expand this list by adding all possible forms in German in the singular and plural, i.e., masculine, feminine, as well as gender-neutral and gender-inclusive alternatives and the English translation. We filter out those that were already neutral, e.g., *"Star"*, which is an Anglicism and does not have variants for other genders in German. Additionally, we remove polysemous terms, e.g., *"aid"*, to facilitate back-translation into English. Our final dictionary counts 115 in their singular and plural forms, containing both professions and common nouns. Ta-

[1] We use the term "gender-fair" to subsume both gender-neutral and inclusive approaches as in Sczesny (2016).

[2] https://geschicktgendern.de/

Proceedings of the 25th Annual Conference of the European Association for Machine Translation (Volume 2), pages 37–38
June 24-27, 2024 ©2024 European Association for Machine Translation

English	MS	MP	FS	FP	GN	GI
The counsellor	Berater	Berater	Beraterin	Beraterinnen	Beratende	der*die Berater*in
The pacifist	Pazifist	Pazifisten	Pazifistin	Pazifistinnen	Friedensbewegte	der*die Pazifist*in

Table 1: Example of the proposed dataset. For each English noun, we collect the German masculine/feminine singular (MS/FS), plural (MP/FP), gender-neutral (GN), and gender-inclusive (GI) forms.

ble 1 reports an example.

(***ii***) In order to test the use of gender-fair language among different systems, we back translate the singular and plural terms in our dataset from English into German with Google Translate, DeepL, GPT-3.5 and GPT-4, and open-weights models, including Opus-MT, FLAN, and Llama models. As a first quantitative inspection, we match the translation outputs with the alternatives in our data set. Next, we conduct a qualitative analysis to gain more insights into the translation of individual terms whose gender is ambiguous with no surrounding context. Subsequently, we investigate the influence of context by collecting and translating sentences that contain our words.

We collect an additional set of English passages that mention our dictionary entries. We sample sentences from Europarl (Koehn, 2005) and Wikipedia.[3] Europarl is a widely recognized benchmark dataset for MT displaying institutional language from parliamentary speeches–perhaps amongst the first contexts GFL was designed for (Piergentili et al., 2023). Wikipedia presents encyclopedic text, opening to new contexts where our seed nouns appear.

(***iii***) Finally, we plan to hire an expert in translation and gender-fair language to create different gender-neutral and inclusive versions of the outputs via post-editing. It will entail gender-neutral rewording, using a gender-inclusive character, e.g. gender star (*), and one or two different neosystems. We will use these outputs as examples to test the few-shot learning capabilities of different Large Language Models (LLMs) for performing gender-fair translation and to develop a gender-fair MT benchmark.

3 Expected Outcome

This project will produce the following openly-accessible resources to the community: **i)** A new human-curated dictionary of English nouns with their German gender-fair inflections. **ii)** A parallel EN-DE corpus with source sentences from Wikipedia and European Parliament speeches that mention the dictionary nouns, and hypothesis sentences automatically translated with several state-of-the-art systems. **iii)** A new human-curated corpus of gender-fair German translations of the sentences above, obtained via post-editing machine-generated translations. Taken together, these resources will constitute the largest collection for studying automatic gender-fair translation from English into German.

Acknowledgments

The GeFMT project (13223) is sponsored by the European Association for Machine Translation (EAMT) under the EAMT Sponsorship of Activities 2023.

References

Koehn, Philipp. 2005. Europarl: A parallel corpus for statistical machine translation. In *Proceedings of Machine Translation Summit X: Papers*, pages 79–86, Phuket, Thailand, September 13-15.

Lardelli, Manuel and Dagmar Gromann. 2023. Gender-fair (machine) translation. In *Proceedings of the New Trends in Translation and Technology Conference - NeTTT 2022*, pages 166–177.

Piergentili, Andrea, Beatrice Savoldi, Dennis Fucci, Matteo Negri, and Luisa Bentivogli. 2023. Hi guys or hi folks? benchmarking gender-neutral machine translation with the GeNTE corpus. In Bouamor, Houda, Juan Pino, and Kalika Bali, editors, *Proceedings of the 2023 Conference on Empirical Methods in Natural Language Processing*, pages 14124–14140, Singapore, December. Association for Computational Linguistics.

Savoldi, Beatrice, Marco Gaido, Luisa Bentivogli, Matteo Negri, and Marco Turchi. 2021. Gender bias in machine translation. *Transactions of the Association for Computational Linguistics*, 9:845–874, 08.

Sczesny, Sabine, Magda Formanowicz, and Franziska Moser. 2016. Can gender-fair language reduce gender stereotyping and discrimination? *Frontiers in Psychology*, 7.

[3] We use the snapshot at 01–03–2022 at `https://huggingface.co/datasets/wikipedia`.

ExU: AI Models for Examining Multilingual Disinformation Narratives and Understanding their Spread

Jake Vasilakes[1], **Zhixue Zhao**[1], **Ivan Vykopal**[2], **Michal Gregor**[2],
Martin Hyben[2], and **Carolina Scarton**[1]

[1] Department of Computer Science, University of Sheffield, UK
[2] Kempelen Institute of Intelligent Technologies, Bratislava, Slovakia
{j.vasilakes, zhixue.zhao, c.scarton}@sheffield.ac.uk
{michal.gregor, ivan.vykopal, martin.hyben}@kinit.sk

1 Project Overview

Online disinformation is a major challenge, with potential to cause economic, social, and medical harm (Zubiaga et al., 2018). Disinformation can be disseminated in multiple languages, which can be an overwhelming challenge for fact-checkers and journalists. It is therefore necessary to develop multilingual methods for analysing disinformation. The ExU project[1] aims to do just that, targeting stance classification and claim retrieval, two central tasks for assisting fact-checkers.

Stance classification predicts whether a piece of content (e.g., a social media post or news article) agrees or disagrees with a claim. Claim retrieval aims to find relevant fact-checks for a given claim. Previous research in these areas, predominantly in English, is largely focused on single languages (Küçük and Can, 2020). Still, there is no research that focuses on developing and evaluating at large-scale a single stance detection or claim retrieval model for multiple languages.

Given these challenges, the objectives of the ExU project are to (1) develop novel methods for multilingual disinformation analysis via the tasks of stance detection and claim retrieval and (2) follow a multilingual user-centric evaluation which focuses on providing explainability of model predictions to end users. Besides English, ExU will work with a set of 20+ languages, providing evaluation frameworks for Portuguese, Spanish, Polish, Slovak, Czech, Hindi and French (languages spoken in the UK and Slovakia). ExU started in November 2023 and is an 18-month project.

[1]https://exuproject.sites.sheffield.ac.uk

2 Progress

We conducted a survey of user requirements for our proposed tools at the Voices Festival of Journalism and Media Literacy,[2] which brings together journalists, fact-checkers, researchers, and educators. Participants were recruited among the visitors to the EMIF (European Media and Information Fund) booth. The survey consisted of 24 questions covering basic demographic information, exposure to multiple languages, and features of stance classification and claim retrieval.

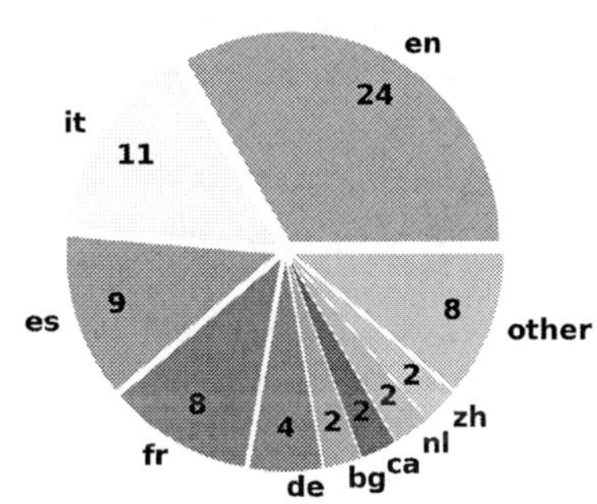

Figure 1: Counts of languages from responses to the survey question "Which languages do you encounter most often in your work?". The "Other" category is comprised of Czech, Hindi, Polish, Portuguese, Russian, Sinhala, Slovak, and Turkish, all of which had a count of one.

We obtained 29 survey responses. Almost all of participants (97%) encountered content in multiple languages when performing fact-checks. Figure 1 indicates the counts of the languages from the participant's answers.[3] For a fact-checking tool in general, participants would like content translated into a language of their choice, so it will be

[2]https://voicesfestival.eu/

[3]The event was held in Florence, Italy, so the results are biased towards EU languages and Italian specifically. We plan to obtain survey data from other demographics in the future.

Proceedings of the 25th Annual Conference of the European Association for Machine Translation (Volume 2), pages 39–40
June 24-27, 2024 ©2024 European Association for Machine Translation

necessary to ensure accuracy of translations both between our target languages and into other user-specified languages. For stance detection, respondents deemed it most important to automatically predict the stance of the post regarding the target claim and to automatically highlight the main argument of posts. For claim retrieval, respondents would like a high-level summary of the claim's fact-checks in addition to the fact-checks themselves.

3 Future work

Based on the initial survey results, we aim for our stance classification models to output accurate and explainable predictions for content across the target languages. Towards this we will utilise multilingual transformers such as Aya (Üstün et al., 2024), which covers all the languages in Figure 1. To address the lack of data for low-resource languages we may obtain small amounts of target language fine-tuning data, as previous work found this improved results (Scarton and Li, 2021). Additionally, we may translate low-resource languages into English before performing classification to leverage the knowledge from English models. We are exploring explainability via feature attribution and rationale extraction, and our preliminary research shows promise for using extractive rationales in multiple languages. Still, explanations ought to be consistent across languages and invariant to translation, yet previous work showed a performance gap in explainability methods between mono- and multi-lingual models (Zhao and Aletras, 2023), so we plan to explore this in depth.

For multilingual claim retrieval, we aim to employ a retrieval augmented generation model (Lewis et al., 2020) to help end users efficiently discern factual claims from debunked ones. This model may facilitate the existing tools for extraction of textual claims from any textual content found online and match them with existing fact-checks contained in our MultiClaim dataset (Pikuliak et al., 2023). The dataset contains 293,169 fact-checked articles and their corresponding claims in 39 languages. The output of the model will include the list of fact-checked claims relevant for each textual claim from the analysed textual content, their language and source references, along with the central claim summarisation of the retrieved claims in natural language.

4 Acknowledgements

The ExU project is funded by the European Media and Information Fund (grant number 291191). The sole responsibility for any content supported by the European Media and Information Fund lies with the author(s) and it may not necessarily reflect the positions of the EMIF and the Fund Partners, the Calouste Gulbenkian Foundation and the European University Institute.

References

Küçük, Dilek and Fazli Can. 2020. Stance detection: A survey. *ACM Computing Surveys*, 53(1):12:1–12:37, February.

Lewis, Patrick, Ethan Perez, Aleksandra Piktus, Fabio Petroni, Vladimir Karpukhin, Naman Goyal, Heinrich Küttler, Mike Lewis, Wen-tau Yih, Tim Rocktäschel, Sebastian Riedel, and Douwe Kiela. 2020. Retrieval-augmented generation for knowledge-intensive NLP tasks. In *Advances in Neural Information Processing Systems*, volume 33, page 9459–9474. Curran Associates, Inc.

Pikuliak, Matús, Ivan Srba, Róbert Móro, Timo Hromadka, Timotej Smolen, Martin Melisek, Ivan Vykopal, Jakub Simko, Juraj Podrouzek, and Mária Bieliková. 2023. Multilingual previously fact-checked claim retrieval. In Bouamor, Houda, Juan Pino, and Kalika Bali, editors, *Proceedings of the 2023 Conference on Empirical Methods in Natural Language Processing, EMNLP 2023, Singapore, December 6-10, 2023*, pages 16477–16500. Association for Computational Linguistics.

Scarton, Carolina and Yue Li. 2021. Cross-lingual rumour stance classification: a first study with BERT and machine translation. In *Truth and Trust Online*, pages 50–59.

Zhao, Zhixue and Nikolaos Aletras. 2023. Incorporating attribution importance for improving faithfulness metrics. In Rogers, Anna, Jordan Boyd-Graber, and Naoaki Okazaki, editors, *Proceedings of the 61st Annual Meeting of the Association for Computational Linguistics (Volume 1: Long Papers)*, pages 4732–4745, Toronto, Canada, July. Association for Computational Linguistics.

Zubiaga, Arkaitz, Ahmet Aker, Kalina Bontcheva, Maria Liakata, and Rob Procter. 2018. Detection and resolution of rumours in social media: A survey. *ACM Computing Surveys*, 51(2):32:1–32:36, February.

Üstün, Ahmet, Viraat Aryabumi, Zheng-Xin Yong, Wei-Yin Ko, Daniel D'souza, Gbemileke Onilude, Neel Bhandari, Shivalika Singh, Hui-Lee Ooi, Amr Kayid, Freddie Vargus, Phil Blunsom, Shayne Longpre, Niklas Muennighoff, Marzieh Fadaee, Julia Kreutzer, and Sara Hooker. 2024. Aya model: An instruction finetuned open-access multilingual language model. *arXiv preprint arXiv:2402.07827*.

Multilinguality in the VIGILANT project

Brendan Spillane[1], Carolina Scarton[2], Robert Moro[3], Petar Ivanov[4], Andrey Tagarev[2,4], Jakub Smiko[3], Ibrahim Abu Farha[2], Gary Munnelly[5], Filip Uhlárik[6], and Freddy Heppell[2]

[1] School of Information and Communication Studies, University College Dublin, Ireland
[2] Department of Computer Science, University of Sheffield, UK
[3] Kempelen Institute of Intelligent Technologies, Bratislava, Slovakia
[4] Sirma AI EAD, Sofia, Bulgaria
[5] School of Computer Science and Statistics, Trinity College Dublin, Ireland
[6] Gerulata Technologies, Bratislava, Slovakia

brendan.spillane@adaptcentre.ie

Abstract

VIGILANT (Vital IntelliGence to Investigate ILlegAl DisiNformaTion)[1] is a three-year Horizon Europe project that will equip European Law Enforcement Agencies (LEAs) with advanced disinformation detection and analysis tools to investigate and prevent criminal activities linked to disinformation. These include disinformation instigating violence towards minorities, promoting false medical cures, and increasing tensions between groups causing civil unrest and violent acts. VIGILANT's four LEAs require support for English, Spanish, Catalan, Greek, Estonian, Romanian and Russian. Therefore, multilinguality is a major challenge and we present the current status of our tools and our plans to improve their performance.

1 Introduction

Disinformation and other related forms of harmful content has an increasingly detrimental effect on society. It is used to reduce trust in healthcare (Naeem et al., 2021), politics and rule of law (Bayer et al., 2019), and influence voting behaviour (Cantarella et al., 2023) or to increase funding and support for criminal networks. It has been classified as a strategic threat to the EU and its member states. Due to its nature, disinformation is extremely difficult for LEAs to identify, investigate and link to criminal activities. The Internet and social media platforms, where anonymity amplifies conspiracy, have provided ideal conditions for it to grow.

Research undertaken in previous projects, e.g. Horizon 2020 PROVENANCE (Yousuf et al., 2021) and WeVerify (Marinova et al., 2020), focused on developing supporting tools for journalists, fact-checkers or to inform the general public about disinformation. Meanwhile, most European LEAs have only recently set-up units to investigate crime related to disinformation. Thus, there is a lack of technical capabilities and institutional knowledge necessary to identify and investigate it. Disinformation that interests LEAs needs to be related to crimes or have the potential to affect the security of citizens. Therefore, general purpose tools do not capture the nuances of these specific cases.

One of the key challenges for VIGILANT is how to provide tools for multiple LEAs in different countries and targetting different languages. The consortium includes LEAs from Greece, Spain, Estonia and Moldova. Therefore, as a minimum, the VIGILANT platform (and its tools) should support: English (EN), Spanish (ES), Catalan (CA), Romanian (RO), Russian (RU), Greek (EL) and Estonian (ET). A Community of Early Adopters (CoEA), which currently has members from Ireland, Spain and Portugal, has been set up for LEAs who are not in the consortium but who wish to adopt VIGILANT. The project aims to provide support for all current and future CoEA required languages to create a common European platform to investigate disinformation linked to criminal activities.

2 Multilingual approaches in VIGILANT

To date, most work in disinformation analysis has been done for English. Developing monolingual approaches for each language from scratch is not feasible, given our project's time-frame and the need for large amounts of data for training state-of-the-art models. Approaches that leverage the

[1] https://www.vigilantproject.eu/

Proceedings of the 25th Annual Conference of the European Association for Machine Translation (Volume 2), pages 41–42
June 24-27, 2024 ©2024 European Association for Machine Translation

Name	EN	ES	ET	CA	EL	RO	RU
Event detection	•	–	–	–	–	–	–
Fact-checked claim detection	•	•	○	•	•	•	○
Central claim detection	•	•	○	○	○	○	○
Synthetic text detection	•	•	○	•	○	○	•
Stance classifier	•	○	○	○	○	○	○
Hate speech detection	•	•	○	○	○	○	○
Multilingual entity linking*	•	•	•	•	•	•	•
Paraphrase-resistant similarity*	•	•	○	○	○	○	•
Narrative analysis*	•	○	○	○	○	○	○

Table 1: VIGILANT tools (• = fine-tuning; ○ = zero-shot; – = no support). * means that the tool is under development.

knowledge learnt in models developed for the English language are thus needed.

Language adaptation in VIGILANT is a challenge for (i) natural language processing (NLP) and information retrieval (IR) tools; (ii) user interface and documentation; and (iii) training materials. We focus on (i), since (ii) and (iii) will be done by LEA professionals.

Multiple tools are being adapted for VIGILANT and here we discuss the challenges for multilingual support and our planned approaches. Table 1 presents a list of NLP and IR tools selected to appear in the VIGILANT platform and their current language support. Most tools support languages other than English in a zero-shot way, i.e., the model is pre-trained on multilingual data, but fine-tuned for the task only on English data. Although creating datasets for fine-tuning models in each language is not feasible, we will aim to create development sets (for domain adaptation) and test sets (to accurately assess whether our tools deliver multilinguality). These should support (i) the languages required by the four LEAs who are partners in the VIGILANT project, (ii) the languages of the members of the CoEA, and ultimately, (iii) as many European languages as possible. They will be created following strict ethical protocols and will be made publicly available when possible.

We will explore multiple approaches for multilingual adaptation:

- Further evaluating the few-shot and zero-shot models capabilities: both for encoder-based (e.g., multilingual BERT) and decoder-based models (e.g., GPT-4).
- Machine translation (MT) of the input to EN to use EN-trained models.
- Using MT for data augmentation and further fine-tuning of our EN-trained models with data in different languages.
- Investigating unsupervised domain adaption techniques, leveraging knowledge from unlabelled monolingual data for adapting our tools to other languages.

3 Project timeline and future work

VIGILANT is 16 months into its 36 month lifespan. In the 1st year of the project, we focused on analysing the tools to be deployed, further developing and adapting their APIs and on developing new tools for image/video and network analysis. We are releasing a minimum viable prototype in 2024 that will integrate NLP and IR tools, supporting EN only. We expect to develop new approaches adapted to multilingual settings in the next 12 months.

Acknowledgements

This work has been co-funded by the EU under the Horizon Europe VIGILANT project, GA No. 101073921 and the Innovate UK (grant 10039039).

References

Bayer, Judit, Natalija Bitiukova, Petra Bard, Judit Szakács, Alberto Alemanno, and Erik Uszkiewicz. 2019. Disinformation and propaganda–impact on the functioning of the rule of law in the eu and its member states. *European Parliament, LIBE Committee, Policy Department for Citizens' Rights and Constitutional Affairs.*

Cantarella, Michele, Nicolò Fraccaroli, and Roberto Volpe. 2023. Does fake news affect voting behaviour? *Research Policy*, 52(1):104628.

Marinova, Zlatina, Jochen Spangenberg, Denis Teyssou, Symeon Papadopoulos, Nikos Sarris, Alexandre Alaphilippe, and Kalina Bontcheva. 2020. Weverify: Wider and enhanced verification for you project overview and tools. In *2020 IEEE International Conference on Multimedia Expo Workshops (ICMEW).*

Naeem, Salman Bin, Rubina Bhatti, and Aqsa Khan. 2021. An exploration of how fake news is taking over social media and putting public health at risk. *Health Information & Libraries Journal*, 38(2):143–149.

Yousuf, Bilal, M. Atif Qureshi, Brendan Spillane, Gary Munnelly, Oisin Carroll, Matthew Runswick, Kirsty Park, Eileen Culloty, Owen Conlan, and Jane Suiter. 2021. Provenance: An intermediary-free solution for digital content verification. In *Proc. of the CIKM 2021 Workshops co-located with 30th ACM Int. Conf. on Inf. and Knowledge Management (CIKM 2021)*, volume 3052. CEUR Workshop Proceedings.

Evaluating Machine Translation for Emotion-loaded User Generated Content (TransEval4Emo-UGC)

Shenbin Qian[1], **Constantin Orăsan**[1], **Félix do Carmo**[1], **Diptesh Kanojia**[2]
[1]Centre for Translation Studies
[2]Institute for People-Centred AI
University of Surrey, UK
{s.qian, c.orasan, f.docarmo, d.kanojia}@surrey.ac.uk

Abstract

This paper presents a dataset for evaluating the machine translation of emotion-loaded user generated content. It contains human-annotated quality evaluation data and post-edited reference translations. The dataset is available at our GitHub repository.[1]

1 Introduction

Machine translation (MT) technology has developed so rapidly in recent years that some claimed to have achieved human parity in Chinese–English news translation (Hassan et al., 2018). Different from news translation, automatically translating user generated content (UGC) has revealed additional challenges for MT systems including handling slang, emotion, literary devices such as irony and sarcasm (Saadany et al., 2023). This is particularly prominent in Chinese social media texts, as various homophones are used to replace offensive words to avoid censorship (Qian et al., 2023).

To evaluate how MT systems perform on emotion-loaded UGC, we collected Chinese microblog texts, and employed Google Translate[2] (GT) to translate them to English. Trained annotators were recruited to directly evaluate translation quality in terms of emotion preservation (through error annotation). Professional translators were hired to post-edit the GT outputs to produce reference translations. Post-edited translations can be used to compare with the MT outputs and to showcase the high-quality translations achievable by human translators. The human evaluation process was funded by the University of Surrey. The post-editing activity was funded by the European Association for Machine Translation (EAMT) through its 2022 sponsorship of student activities.

2 Data Description

This project delivered a dataset comprising 5538 instances of Chinese microblog texts (source), their machine-translated English versions, information on human-annotated errors and quality evaluation scores (QEval information), and post-edited translations (reference).

2.1 Source

The source originated from the dataset released by the *Evaluation of Weibo Emotion Classification Technology on the Ninth China National Conference on Social Media Processing* (SMP2020-EWECT). The original dataset was sourced from *Weibo*,[3] the largest microblogging platform in China. It has a size of 34,768 instances. Each instance is a tweet-like text segment, which was manually annotated with one of the six emotion labels, i.e., *anger*, *joy*, *sadness*, *surprise*, *fear* and *neutral* (Guo et al., 2021). We selected a random sample of 5538 instances (20%) with non-neutral emotion labels as our primary resource to examine how MT renders emotion-loaded UGC.

2.2 QEval information

Two annotators with Chinese–English translation qualifications were recruited to evaluate the quality of these GT outputs in terms of emotion preservation. The evaluation employs the Multi-dimensional Quality Metrics (MQM) framework (Lommel et al., 2014), to assess the translation quality across various error dimensions like

[1]https://github.com/surrey-nlp/HADQAET for data & licence

[2]https://translate.google.co.uk/ on the 30th of May, 2022

[3]https://weibo.com/

Proceedings of the 25th Annual Conference of the European Association for Machine Translation (Volume 2), pages 43–44
June 24-27, 2024 ©2024 European Association for Machine Translation

accuracy, fluency, terminology, and more. We introduced a modified framework inspired by MQM to annotate error types and severity levels related to emotion preservation. The output of this process is human-annotated errors and their corresponding severity levels for each of these 5538 instances. Details for the new MQM-based framework, error annotations (including annotation guidelines and inter-annotator agreement), error analysis and data distribution can be seen in Qian et al (2023).

These errors can be used to calculate a quality evaluation (QEval) score based on the weight assigned to each severity level. This score represents the human assessment of the MT quality in terms of emotion preservation. The words that cause the errors were also annotated as wrong/bad translations, which can provide insights into translation quality at word level. QEval scores and error annotations can be utilized to train machine learning systems. These systems can then predict similar scores and word annotations, offering a way to approximate human evaluation in the absence of a gold standard.

2.3 Reference

We hired a translation company to post-edit 2778 instances of the GT output. These instances were identified as having errors related to emotion preservation during the quality evaluation process. Before the post-editing process starts, the translators received clear instructions that: 1) the task involves the post-editing of the provided GT translations, and 2) maintaining the source's emotion is just as crucial as conveying its meaning. They were given enough time (approximately one month) to complete the job to avoid fatigue and ensure quality. The post-edited translations were delivered in two batches for quality checks using random sampling.

While training quality estimation systems can serve as a proxy for quality evaluation (Specia et al., 2018), the system performance improves when human-translated references are accessible (Wan et al., 2022). These high-quality reference translations are valuable for comparing machine translation and training automatic QEval systems.

3 Conclusion

To our best knowledge, this dataset is the first open-sourced Chinese–English resource in the MT area that includes human-annotated translation errors, words that cause the errors, quality evaluation scores in terms of emotion preservation, post-edited reference translations, and emotion labels. We believe it is valuable for the evaluation of translation quality for emotion-loaded UGC, and for the training of new MT systems.

References

Guo, Xianwei, Hua Lai, Yan Xiang, Zhengtao Yu, and Yuxin Huang. 2021. Emotion Classification of COVID-19 Chinese Microblogs based on the Emotion Category Description. pages 916–927. Chinese Information Processing Society of China, August.

Hassan, Hany, Anthony Aue, Chang Chen, Vishal Chowdhary, Jonathan Clark, Christian Federmann, Xuedong Huang, Marcin Junczys-Dowmunt, William Lewis, Mu Li, Shujie Liu, Tie-Yan Liu, Renqian Luo, Arul Menezes, Tao Qin, Frank Seide, Xu Tan, Fei Tian, Lijun Wu, Shuangzhi Wu, Yingce Xia, Dongdong Zhang, Zhirui Zhang, and Ming Zhou. 2018. Achieving Human Parity on Automatic Chinese to English News Translation. *arXive preprint*.

Lommel, Arle Richard, Aljoscha Burchardt, and Hans Uszkoreit. 2014. Multidimensional Quality Metrics: A Flexible System for Assessing Translation Quality. *Tradumàtica: tecnologies de la traducció*, 12:455–463, December.

Qian, Shenbin, Constantin Orasan, Felix Do Carmo, Qiuliang Li, and Diptesh Kanojia. 2023. Evaluation of Chinese-English machine translation of emotion-loaded microblog texts: A human annotated dataset for the quality assessment of emotion translation. In *Proceedings of the 24th Annual Conference of the European Association for Machine Translation*, pages 125–135, Tampere, Finland, June. European Association for Machine Translation.

Saadany, Hadeel, Constantin Orasan, Rocio Caro Quintana, Felix Do Carmo, and Leonardo Zilio. 2023. Analysing mistranslation of emotions in multilingual tweets by online MT tools. In *Proceedings of the 24th Annual Conference of the European Association for Machine Translation*, pages 275–284, Tampere, Finland, June. European Association for Machine Translation.

Specia, Lucia, Caroline Scarton, and Gustavo Henrique Paetzold. 2018. *Quality Estimation for Machine Translation*. Morgan Claypool.

Wan, Yu, Dayiheng Liu, Baosong Yang, Haibo Zhang, Boxing Chen, Derek Wong, and Lidia Chao. 2022. UniTE: Unified translation evaluation. In *Proceedings of the 60th Annual Meeting of the Association for Computational Linguistics (Volume 1: Long Papers)*, pages 8117–8127, Dublin, Ireland, May. Association for Computational Linguistics.

Community-driven machine translation for the Catalan language at Softcatalà

Xavi Ivars-Ribes, Jordi Mas, Marc Riera Jaume Ortolà, David Cànovas
Softcatalà
{xavivars,jmas,marcriera,
jaumeortola,davidcanovas}
@softcatala.org

Mikel L. Forcada
Softcatalà and
Prompsit Language Engineering
mlf@prompsit.com

Abstract

Among the services provided by Softcatalà, a non-profit 25-year-old grassroots organization that localizes software into Catalan and develops software to ease the generation of Catalan content, one of the most used is its machine translation (MT) service, which provides both rule-based MT and neural MT between Catalan and twelve other languages. Development occurs in a community-supported, transparent way by using free/open-source software and open language resources. This paper briefly describes the MT services at Softcatalà: the offered functionalities, the data, and the software used to provide them.

1 Introduction

Softcatalà[1] is a non-profit organization dedicated to promoting the use of Catalan in the realm of computing, internet, and new technologies. This organization leverages a volunteer workforce composed of computer specialists, philologists, translators, students, and others. These volunteers contribute to the translation of software interfaces and documentation into Catalan, while also developing tools that facilitate the creation and use of Catalan-language content.

In addition to a long history of providing Catalan-localized versions of popular software, Softcatalà offers a number of web-based documentation and language-related services, such as a grammar and spelling checker for Catalan, a video and audio transcription service, or machine translation (MT) systems. The service is mainly ad-supported, free to use, and very popular in the Catalan language community.[2] This paper describes Softcatalà's MT service: the functionalities offered, the data, and the software used to provide them.

2 The service

Softcatalà's MT service[3] provides MT between Catalan and Aragonese, Occitan (both Aranese and Languedocian), French, English, Italian and Spanish using the free/open-source rule-based MT platform Apertium, and between Catalan and Dutch, English, French, Galician, German, Italian, Japanese, Portuguese, and Romanian using neural MT. Most of our users are students, teachers, and public workers.

3 The inner workings

3.1 Rule-based machine translation

The rule-based MT systems powering Softcatalà's machine translation services are all based on the free/open-source machine translation platform Apertium (Forcada et al., 2011).[4] The first such service, between Catalan and Spanish, was launched in 2010[5] (Ivars-Ribes and Sánchez-Cartagena, 2011). Softcatalà has contributed massively to this platform, particularly by improving the language data (dictionaries, rules) and the configuration of the MT pipelines used for language pairs involving Catalan. Due to the commitment of key Softcatalà developers as part of the Apertium community, their contributions soon propagate to other services based on Apertium, improving their performance; for instance, SALT.usu, the official Spanish↔Valencian[6] MT system of the Valencian

[1] https://www.softcatala.org

[2] More than 220,000 translations/day in 2023.

[3] https://www.softcatala.org/traductor/

[4] https://apertium.org

[5] Previously, the (now extinct) machine translation service interNOSTRUM was offered since 2000.

[6] Valencian is the name given in the Valencia region to the local variety of Catalan; in writing, the standards used in Valen-

Proceedings of the 25th Annual Conference of the European Association for Machine Translation (Volume 2), pages 45–46
June 24-27, 2024 ©2024 European Association for Machine Translation

regional government. Anyone can install these improved systems locally off the Apertium webpage.

3.2 Neural machine translation

Softcatalà's neural MT systems[7] use the `OpenNMT-tf`[8] sequence learning toolkit, which in turn is based on TensorFlow[9] version 2; they are trained on publicly-available parallel corpora,[10] using a publicly documented training procedure;[11] all text-processing and training software is free/open-source. Trained models[12] and Docker containers are available for anyone to download and deploy in their own servers. Memory- and speed-optimized models (using `CTranslate2`[13]) are also provided, which allow for CPU-only inference and therefore produce a smaller CO_2 footprint during inference.

4 Evaluation

In Table 1 we report the latest automatic evaluation results (BLEU using SacreBLEU's default 13a tokenization (Post, 2018)) for Softcatalà's MT systems, and a comparison with Google Translate, Meta's NLLB model `nllb-200-3.3B`, and Opus-MT,[14] using the Flores200 test set.[15]

Note that the results correspond to models used in production with modest hardware (CPU), which strike a balance between accuracy and speed; BLEU could be improved with slower models. Also note that Flores200 was produced translating from English to many of the other languages, and that means that in language pairs not containing English, say, `pt–ca`, sentence pairs are quite different from what would be obtained if translating directly from `pt` to `ca`; results have therefore to be taken with additional caution.

As can be seen in Table 1, the BLEU scores obtained by Softcatalà's systems, when evaluated against Flores 200: (a) are consistently better than Opus-MT's freely-available models; (b) lag well behind Google Translate, a much larger commercial model for most pairs, but get quite close to it for `es–ca`, `ca–es`, `ca–gl`, and `en–ca`; (c) are competitive compared to those by Meta's much larger NLLB model. Note that Google regularly updates their MT models; the results shown are about one year old (for details, see `https://github.com/Softcatala/nmt-models`). We plan to publish additional metrics in the next training round.

Pair	SC	F200	Goo	NLLB	Opus	Sent. pairs
de–ca	34.8	28.9	35.5	30.7	18.5	3142257
ca–de	28.5	25.4	32.9	29.1	15.8	3142257
en–ca	46.9	43.8	46.0	41.7	29.8	7856208
ca–en	47.4	43.5	47.0	48.0	29.6	7856208
fr–ca	41.3	31.6	37.3	33.3	27.2	2566302
ca–fr	41.4	35.4	41.7	39.6	27.9	2566302
gl–ca	74.1	31.4	36.5	33.2	N/A	2710149
ca–gl	80.7	31.9	33.1	31.7	N/A	2710149
it–ca	39.7	26.5	30.6	27.8	22.0	2584598
ca–it	36.2	24.5	27.5	26.0	19.2	2584598
ja–ca	24.9	17.8	23.4	N/A	N/A	1997740
ca–ja	21.3	19.8	32.5	N/A	N/A	1997740
nl–ca	30.4	20.3	27.1	24.8	15.8	2208538
ca–nl	27.6	18.2	23.4	21.8	13.4	2208538
oc–ca	74.9	32.5	N/A	36.2	N/A	2711350
ca–oc	78.8	28.9	N/A	27.8	N/A	2711350
pt–ca	41.6	33.9	38.7	34.5	28.1	2043019
ca–pt	39.0	32.3	40.0	36.5	27.5	2043019
es–ca	88.8	22.6	23.6	25.8	22.5	7596985
ca–es	87.5	24.2	24.2	25.5	23.2	7596985

Table 1: BLEU scores for the latest versions of Softcatalà's (SC's) MT systems. **SC**: SC using SC's own test sets; `F200`: SC using the Flores 200 test set; `Goo`, `NLLB` and `Opus-MT`: results of these three systems using the Flores200 test set.

5 Concluding remarks

The community-driven effort of Softcatalà, a grassroots organization devoted to digitally enable the Catalan language, has managed to provide the community with competitive, freely-available, open machine translation systems that anyone can use or even improve using free/open-source software.

References

Forcada, Mikel L, Mireia Ginestí-Rosell, Jacob Nordfalk, Jim O'Regan, Sergio Ortiz-Rojas, Juan Antonio Pérez-Ortiz, Felipe Sánchez-Martínez, Gema Ramírez-Sánchez, and Francis M Tyers. 2011. Apertium: a free/open-source platform for rule-based machine translation. *Machine translation*, 25:127–144.

Ivars-Ribes, Xavier and Victor M. Sánchez-Cartagena. 2011. A widely used machine translation service and its migration to a free/open-source solution: the case of softcatalà. In *Proceedings of the Second International Workshop on Free/Open-Source Rule-Based Machine Translation*, pages 61–68, Barcelona.

Post, Matt. 2018. A call for clarity in reporting BLEU scores. In *Proceedings of the Third Conference on Machine Translation: Research Papers*, pages 186–191, Brussels, Belgium.

cia and Catalonia or the Balearic Islands are not too different.

[7] `https://github.com/Softcatala/nmt-softcatala`

[8] `https://github.com/OpenNMT/OpenNMT-tf`

[9] `https://www.tensorflow.org/`

[10] `https://github.com/Softcatala/parallel-corpus`

[11] `https://github.com/Softcatala/nmt-models/`

[12] `https://github.com/Softcatala/nmt-models/`

[13] `https://github.com/OpenNMT/CTranslate2`

[14] `https://github.com/Helsinki-NLP/Opus-MT`

[15] `https://github.com/facebookresearch/flores`

The MTxGames Project: Creative Video Games and Machine Translation – Different Post-Editing Methods in the Translation Process

Judith Brenner
University of Eastern Finland
School of Humanities
Yliopistokatu 2, 80100 Joensuu, Finland
jbrenner@uef.fi

Abstract

MTxGames is a doctoral research project examining three different machine translation (MT) post-editing (PE) methods in the context of translating creative texts from video games, focusing on translation speed, cognitive effort, quality, and translators' preferences. This is a mixed-methods study, eliciting quantitative data through keylogging, eye-tracking, and error evaluation as well as qualitative data through interviews. To create realistic experimental conditions, data elicitation takes place at the workplaces of freelancing professional game translators.

1 Introduction

In terms of revenue, the global video games market has been growing for more than a decade (Wijman, 2024). Due to this growth, more and more texts in and about video games need to be translated in ever shorter periods of time (Anselmi and Rubio, 2020). Rising volumes, increasingly tighter deadlines, and the emerging popularity of generative artificial intelligence (AI) in tech-savvy fields have led to more interest by game publishers and developers in applying MT to speed up the translation processes, either in the form of dedicated neural machine translation (NMT) systems or large language models (LLMs) prompted for MT. However, as their multi-modal features and creative characteristics make game texts more complex compared to other text types, PE of NMT suggestions may have counter effects when translating creative texts. For example, Guerberof Arenas and Toral (2022) found that PE might reduce productivity and hinder the creative process. Instead of post-editing MT suggestions, novel approaches for using MT in video game translation are needed that take these creative aspects into account.

Additionally, there might be differences for each individual game translator. Prior research on (statistical) MT has found, for example, individual differences in PE productivity (Koehn and Germann, 2014) and personal preferences (Daems, 2016). Considering recent technological advancements, MTxGames aims to investigate how PE practices can be adapted to accelerate the process of translating video games while maintaining high-quality, creative translations and accommodating for translators' preferences regarding the use of NMT and LLMs. Therefore, three PE methods are compared against each other: 1) Traditional post-editing, where pre-translated machine-generated texts are provided by an NMT system customised for game texts and which are then post-edited by the translator. 2) MT-assisted translation without pre-translation, allowing the translator to pull suggestions for individual sentences from a customised NMT system on demand. 3) Interactive MT, which involves the translator to prompt an LLM for a translation which can then be further fine-tuned through more prompting. While 1) is prevalent in video game translation, 2) is rare, and 3) is still a novel concept requiring further development.

By focusing on the translator's point of view, this project represents a shift in MT research and moves the field toward human-centred augmented translation as proposed by O'Brien (2023).

2 The Project

This doctoral research is affiliated with University of Eastern Finland in cooperation with Technische Hochschule Köln (TH Köln – University of Applied Sciences), Germany. The project started in January 2022 and is expected to take four years. A personal grant by the Finnish Kone Foundation was awarded for three years, from 2023 to 2025 (project number 202202303). Data elicitation is funded by the EAMT Sponsorship of Activities, Students' Edition 2023, covering expenses for travel to participants' offices.

Proceedings of the 25th Annual Conference of the European Association for Machine Translation (Volume 2), pages 47–48
June 24-27, 2024 ©2024 European Association for Machine Translation

MTxGames is realised in collaboration with two industry partners that are localisation service providers for the video games industry, who have asked to remain unnamed at the current stage of the project. These industry partners provide resources such as setting up realistic projects in the translation management system of choice (memoQ), access to their production-ready MT system customised for game texts,[1] a pool of freelancers for recruiting study participants, source texts from a real game localisation project as well as well-maintained translation memories and terminology databases.

3 Data Elicitation and Analysis

To ensure comparability of the three PE methods, all participants work with the same game texts unknown to them at the time of the experiment. The game texts are selected based on their units of creative potential as described by Guerberof Arenas and Toral (2020). The source language is English, the target languages French, Italian, German, and Spanish, representing the main target languages of the industry partners.

Researchers of eye-tracking studies point out that translation process research in the translator's typical work environment leads to more realistic insights (Macken et al., 2020; Saldanha and O'Brien, 2014; Teixeira and O'Brien, 2018). Therefore, data elicitation is conducted in the offices of the study participants, who are freelancing professional video game translators. This way they are observed in the work environment they are used to, with their usual equipment, ambient temperature, and background noises, eliminating environmental disturbance factors, and with as minimal changes to their usual work as possible. Due to research constraints, the number of study participants is limited to 10–12. While this does not result in sufficient data for an inferential statistical analysis, it allows uncovering causal mechanisms between the translation condition and the factors of temporal and cognitive effort, quality, and preference.

Temporal and cognitive effort as well as quality are measured quantitatively and analysed descriptively, and the translators' preferences are measured and analysed qualitatively. To determine temporal effort, keylogging gives exact edit times for each translation segment. Cognitive effort is derived from gaze fixations gathered by eye-tracking, as several scholars have shown that gaze fixations are indicators for cognitive effort (see Saldanha and O'Brien, 2014). Quality is measured by the number and types of errors in the post-edited translation, based on the MQM (Multidimensional Quality Metrics) framework[2] tailored to the specific requirements for a high-quality, creative game translation. Additionally, a spot check of the MT output helps to understand whether errors originated in the MT output or were introduced by the translator. The fourth factor, preference, is measured by conducting interviews with all study participants. These interviews cover subjective perception of the PE method's usefulness, resulting quality, and productivity-enhancing capabilities. Methodological triangulation of objective data and subjective perception is expected to lead to strong insights on which PE method is favourable for productive, satisfied translators who produce quality game translations.

References

Anselmi, Cristina and Inés Rubio. 2020. The Future is Here: Neural Machine Translation for Games. *MultiLingual* 31(2):40–45.

Daems, Joke. 2016. *A Translation Robot for each Translator? A Comparative Study of Manual Translation and Post-editing of Machine Translations: Process, Quality and Translator Attitude*. Ghent University. Faculty of Arts and Philosophy. Dissertation. http://hdl.handle.net/1854/LU-8058017.

Guerberof Arenas, Ana and Antonio Toral. 2020. The Impact of Post-editing and Machine Translation on Creativity and Reading Experience. *Translation Spaces*, 9(2):255–282.

Guerberof Arenas, Ana and Antonio Toral. 2022. Creativity in Translation: Machine Translation as a Constraint for Literary Texts. *Translation Spaces*, 11(2): 184–212.

Koehn, Philipp and Ulrich Germann. 2014. The Impact of Machine Translation Quality on Human Post-editing. In Ulrich Germann et al. (eds.). *Proceedings of the EACL 2014 Workshop on Humans and Computer-assisted Translation*: 38–46. Association for Computational Linguistics.

Macken, Lieve, Daniel Prou, and Arda Tezcan. 2020. Quantifying the Effect of Machine Translation in a High-Quality Human Translation Production Process. *Informatics* 7(2): 12.

Newzoo. 2024. Games Market Trends to watch in 2024. Technical report. https://newzoo.com/resources/trend-reports/games-market-trends-to-watch-in-2024.

O'Brien, Sharon. 2023. Human-Centered Augmented Translation: Against Antagonistic Dualisms. *Perspectives.*

Saldanha, Gabriela and Sharon O'Brien. 2014. *Research Methodologies in Translation Studies.* Routledge.

Teixeira, Carlos S. C. and Sharon O'Brien. 2018. *Overcoming Methodological Challenges of Eye Tracking in the Translation Workplace.* In Callum Walker and Federico M. Federici. Eye Tracking and Multidisciplinary Studies on Translation. John Benjamins.

[1] The decision for the MT system will be made after submitting this paper but before the EAMT conference in June 2024.

[2] https://themqm.org/

SignON – a Co-creative Machine Translation for Sign and Spoken Languages (end-of-project results, contributions and lessons learned)

Dimitar Shterionov[*], **Vincent Vandeghinste**[†a], **Mirella De Sisto**[*], **Aoife Brady**[‡], **Mathieu De Coster**[§]
Lorraine Leeson[¶], **Josep Blat**[**], **Frankie Picron**[††], **Davy Van Landuyt**[††], **Marcello Paolo Scipioni**[‡‡]
Andy Way[‡], **Aditya Parikh**[§§], **Louis ten Bosch**[§§], **John O'Flaherty**[‖], **Joni Dambre**[§], **Caro Brosens**[x],
Jorn Rijckaert[x], **Bram Vanroy**[a], **Victor Ubieto Nogales**[**], **Santiago Egea Gomez**[**], **Ineke Schuurman**[a]
Gorka Labaka[b], **Adrián Núñez-Marcos**[b], **Irene Murtagh**[c], **Euan McGill**[**], **Horacio Saggion**[**]
[*]Tilburg University, [†]Instituut voor de Nederlandse Taal, [‡]ADAPT, [§]Ghent University,
[¶]Trinity College Dublin,[**]Universitat Pompeu Fabra,[††]European Union of the Deaf,
[‡‡]Fincons,[§§]Radboud University,[‖]mac.ie,[x]Vlaams Gebarentaalcentrum, [a]KU Leuven,
[b]University of the Basque Country UPV/EHU, [c]TU Dublin

SignON,[1] a 3-year Horizon 2020[2] project addressing the lack of technology and services for MT between sign languages (SLs) and spoken languages (SpLs) ended in December 2023. SignON was unprecedented. Not only it addressed the wider complexity of the aforementioned problem – from research and development of recognition, translation and synthesis, through development of easy-to-use mobile applications and a cloud-based framework to do the "heavy lifting" as well as to establishing ethical, privacy and inclusiveness policies and operation guidelines – but also engaged with the deaf and hard of hearing communities in an effective co-creation approach where these main stakeholders drove the development in the right direction and had the final say.

Currently we are witnessing advances in natural language processing for SLs, including MT. SignON was one of the largest projects that contributed to this surge with 17 partners and more than 60 consortium members, working in parallel with other international and European initiatives, such as project EASIER[3] and others.

SignON MT – framework SignON set out to develop an MT service supporting 4 SpLs (Dutch, Spanish, Irish and English) in both written and spoken forms and 5 SLs (Sign Language of the Netherlands (NGT), Flemish Sign Language (VGT), Spanish Sign Language (LSE), Irish Sign Language (ISL) and British Sign Language (BSL)) in any possible direction. A fleet of dedicated language-pair-specific models would be infeasible. Considering the unsustainable nature of such an approach SignON employed a divide-and-conquer strategy splitting the task into automatic speech recognition (ASR) and sign language recognition (SLR), MT and synthesis. The MT core we built (i.e. the *InterL*) is based on mBART (Lewis et al., 2020) and on symbolic representations and aims to capture the meaning of all languages (spoken and signed) and to facilitate the translation processes; ASR and SLR components provide input to the InterL – text in the case of ASR and visual and temporal embeddings for SLR; text outputs from InterL is displayed to the user or fed into an SLS and a text-to-speech component to generate the target language utterance in the targeted modality.

SignON – Co-creation Up till SignON commenced, SLMT work lacked the proper inclusion of deaf and hard of hearing people in the process of planning projects, participating as equal partners in researching, and responding to work in development stage (Bragg et al., 2019).

To address the aforementioned gap, the SignON project involved the deaf and hard of hearing communities from the beginning. First, two deaf-led organisations were involved from the inception stage with leading roles within the consortium. Second, SignON employed a co-creation approach which places deaf and hard of hearing stakeholders at the centre of the design process. We defined co-creation as *a collaboration between researchers, developers and users, based on continuous, periodic information exchange, expectation management, openness and user-involvement (in the design and development process), on equal merits and built on trust, from the project inception.* We conducted 12 co-creation events and surveys spread over duration of the project and ge-

[1] `https://signon-project.eu/`
[2] RIA Grant Agreement No. 101017255
[3] `https://project-easier.eu/`

Proceedings of the 25th Annual Conference of the European Association for Machine Translation (Volume 2), pages 49–50
June 24-27, 2024 ©2024 European Association for Machine Translation

ographically over the regions of every involved language. Co-creation events included interviews, round tables and workshops. Following analysis of the collected feedback, information was fed into the development cycle which, ultimately, led to 3 major releases (of the SignON MT App).

SignON – an open and sustainable solution The SignON services involve various models, tools and components that are deployed on a distributed framework. Code, models and documentation are available on github (`https://github.com/signon-project`) and huggingface (`https://huggingface.co/signon-project`). Public deliverables, which describe the SignON outputs and outcomes are available at `https://signon-project.eu/publications/public-deliverables/`. The availability of code, models, documentation and data is only one side of the sustainability dimension of SignON. Alongside the translation pipelines, we have embedded a learning/training aspect. In particular, (i) we built pipelines to easily adapt models to new data and (ii) more importantly, alongside the translation app we developed a data collection app which allows the collection of user-generated data.

The wide span of SignON led to many satellite initiatives. Two of these, ELE- and EAMT-funded projects (De Sisto et al., 2023a; De Sisto et al., 2023b), focused on data collection, as data (or the lack of it) is one of the main challenges uncovered in SignON. In particular, the data-related problems include insufficient (for deep learning) volumes of data, formatting and difficulties with processing of data,[4] quality of the data (Vandeghinste et al., forthcoming), and even related to data authenticity i.e. most of the data is generated by hearing interpreters who can be considered L2 signers but also translating under time pressure, leading to "translationese". These two projects led to the generation of two CC-BY NC and CC-BY licensed datasets, available or soon to be available through CLARIN[5] and the ELG,[6] aiming to further the development of NLP for SLs. Other SignON data is distributed through the CLARIN infrastructure and is listed in: `https://www.clarin.eu/resource-families/sign-language-resources`.

[4]As noted in (Morgan et al., 2022; Vandeghinste et al., 2023) while the majority of the SL data is stored as videos, no automatic annotation tool is available, requiring manual work.

[5]`http://hdl.handle.net/10032/tm-a2-x5`, `http://hdl.handle.net/10032/tm-a2-x4`, `http://hdl.handle.net/10032/tm-a2-x6`

[6]`https://live.european-language-grid.eu/catalogue/corpus/21535`, `https://live.european-languagegrid.eu/catalogue/corpus/23007`

References

Bragg, Danielle, Oscar Koller, Mary Bellard, Larwan Berke, Patrick Boudreault, Annelies Braffort, Naomi Caselli, Matt Huenerfauth, Hernisa Kacorri, Tessa Verhoef, Christian Vogler, and Meredith Ringel Morris. 2019. Sign language recognition, generation, and translation: An interdisciplinary perspective. In *ASSETS 2019 – 21st International ACM SIGACCESS Conference on Computers and Accessibility*, pages 16–31.

De Sisto, Mirella, Dimitar Shterionov, Lien Soetemans, Vincent Vandeghinste, and Caro Brosens. 2023a. Ngt-horeco and gost-parc-sign: Two new sign language - spoken language parallel corpora. In Krister Lindén, Jyrki Niemi and Thalassia Kontino, editors, *CLARIN Annual Conference Proceedings*, Leuven, Belgium.

De Sisto, Mirella, Vincent Vandeghinste, Lien Soetemans, Caro Brosens, and Dimitar Shterionov. 2023b. GoSt-ParC-sign: Gold standard parallel corpus of sign and spoken language. In Nurminen, Mary, Judith Brenner, Maarit Koponen, Sirkku Latomaa, Mikhail Mikhailov, Frederike Schierl, Tharindu Ranasinghe, Eva Vanmassenhove, Sergi Alvarez Vidal, Nora Aranberri, Mara Nunziatini, Carla Parra Escartín, Mikel Forcada, Maja Popovic, Carolina Scarton, and Helena Moniz, editors, *Proceedings of the 24th Annual Conference of the European Association for Machine Translation*, pages 503–504, Tampere, Finland, June. European Association for Machine Translation.

Lewis, Mike, Yinhan Liu, Naman Goyal, Marjan Ghazvininejad, Abdelrahman Mohamed, Omer Levy, Veselin Stoyanov, and Luke Zettlemoyer. 2020. BART: denoising sequence-to-sequence pre-training for natural language generation, translation, and comprehension. In D. Jurafsky et al., editor, *Proc. of the 58th Annual Meeting of the Assoc. for Computational Linguistics, ACL 2020, Online, July 5-10, 2020*, pages 7871–7880. ACL.

Morgan, Hope E., Onno Crasborn, Maria Kopf, Marc Schulder, and Thomas Hanke. 2022. Facilitating the spread of new sign language technologies across Europe. In Efthimiou, Eleni, Stavroula-Evita Fotinea, Thomas Hanke, Julie A. Hochgesang, Jette Kristoffersen, Johanna Mesch, and Marc Schulder, editors, *Proceedings of the LREC2022 10th workshop on the representation and processing of sign languages: Multilingual sign language resources*, pages 144–147, Marseille, France. European Language Resources Association (ELRA).

Vandeghinste, Vincent, Mirella De Sisto, Maria Kopf, Marc Schulder, Caro Brosens, Lien Soetemans, Rehana Omardeen, Frankie Picron, Davy Van Landuyt, Irene Murtagh, Elefterios Avramidis, and Mathieu De Coster. 2023. Report on Europe's Sign Languages. Technical report, European Language Equality D1.40.

Vandeghinste, Vincent, Mirella De Sisto, Santiago Egea Gómez, and Mathieu De Coster. forthcoming. Challenges with sign language datasets.

The Use of MT in Humanitarian NGOs in Hong Kong

Marija Todorova
Hong Kong Baptist University
todorova@hkbu.edu.hk

Rachel Hang Yi Liu
Hong Kong Baptist University
rachelhyliu@hkbu.edu.hk

Abstract

In the relief operations of international humanitarian organisations, non-governmental organisations (NGOs) often encounter language needs when delivering services (Tesseur 2022). This project examines the language needs of humanitarian NGOs working in international disaster relief from Hong Kong and the solutions they adopted to overcome the language barriers when delivering international humanitarian aid to other countries.

1 Project Overview

Providing development aid in international settings requires adaptation to the diverse environments as one of the key components to the daily operation of development organisations. In these settings, translation is one of the most important tools at the disposal of development organisations, as they seek to engage with their local partners, volunteers, beneficiaries, and marginalised groups. This proposed research project will focus on the use of translation, including MT, in emergencies and within the humanitarian aspects of development aid, or more specifically, humanitarian aid provided by International humanitarian NGOs in Hong Kong to victims of disaster in other countries.

The research project is titled *Examining Translation and Interpreting as Inclusion: Language Use in Hong Kong's Development Aid to Africa*. The project started in January 2024 and will last for 24 months. The principal investigator is from Hong Kong Baptist University, while the coinvestigators are from University of Geneva and Free State University, South Africa.

The ways of disseminating information across language barriers have been revolutionised by the emergence of Machine Translation. This study investigates how humanitarian NGOs tackled the linguistic challenges in Hong Kong. From the preliminary results collected with a survey of Hong Kong humanitarian NGOs, it is found that Machine Translation is one of the solutions they adopted for their operations. Machine Translation refers to the automatic conversion of text from one language to another with which grammatical structure and meaning are preserved (Hutchins & Somers, 1992). Professional translations require processing time and extra fee; for organisations that do not include a budget for translation, open-access machine translation is one of the alternatives to professional translation.

Project Aims

This study aims to investigate the impact of linguistic problems in Hong Kong's international development and crisis responses sectors and their language approaches applied to their work with the following aims:

1. To understand the translation needs of humanitarian NGOs in Hong Kong,
2. To analyse the impact of the solutions adopted by these NGOs, including MT, and
3. To advise more inclusive translation and interpreting policies and practices within Hong Kong humanitarian organizations, especially towards the most vulnerable beneficiaries.

Proceedings of the 25th Annual Conference of the European Association for Machine Translation (Volume 2), pages 51–52
June 24-27, 2024 ©2024 European Association for Machine Translation

2 Research and Methodology

In the first instance the research is conducted by a survey of humanitarian organisations in Hong Kong which had received Disaster Relief Fund in the past 5 years to understand the practice of tackling language challenges by these NGOs .

Furthermore, a survey will be conducted with recipients of humanitarian relief in Malawi in order to gain insight into the use of translation in order to negotiate aid distribution priorities in the local community and establish meaningful relations with the local population, majority of whom use a number of indigenous languages, with Chewa being the most widely spoken national language, followed by Yao, Sena, and Tonga.

3 Results and Discussion

From the 11 initial responses received from 9 NGOs that had received Disaster Relief Fund, it is found that Cantonese (traditional Chinese) and English are the mostly used languages at work. Some of the humanitarian workers reported that they possessed other language ability but not the languages spoken in relief areas which indicates that direction communication between Hong Kong Offices and the beneficiaries is impossible if the relief areas are non-English speaking.

Only less than 20% of organisations hired professional translators. As can be seen from the survey results, humanitarian organisations in Hong Kong do not have translation teams and translation policies in place, and professional translators are rarely engaged to provide translation services. This corresponds with the findings from other international humanitarian organisations (Federici et al. 2019). The data showed that around 65% of the respondents' work routine involves translation, in which 80% of them used Google Translate and 60% of them used online dictionaries as technical support for the translation. The result verified the translation demands within humanitarian NGOs but the solution to the demand is usually resolved by the staff on their own. Regarding the workflow, all respondents who worked in overseas relief areas communicate with their beneficiaries through local partners and contact person that can speak local languages; this reflects the reliance on local contact persons when providing assistance and support for relief areas in these NGOs.

Based on the results, the implications of using MT in humanitarian organisations will be discussed. Some of the issues include:

- **Implications of the Use of MT in humanitarian NGOs**
- **Necessity of standardising the TM in humanitarian organisations**
- **Training of using MT - post editing and evaluation for humanitarian use**

Acknowledgement

This work was supported by the University Grants Committee of Hong Kong, General Research Fund, grant number 12608623.

References

Cadwell, P., O'Brien, S., & DeLuca, E. (2019). A critical reflection on developing and testing crisis machine translation technology. Translation Spaces, 8(2), 300-333.

Federici, F.M., Declercq, C., Cintas, J.D., Piñero, R.B. (2023). Ethics, Automated Processes, Machine Translation, and Crises. In H. Moniz & C. Parra Escartín (eds) Towards Responsible Machine Translation. Machine Translation: Technologies and Applications. Springer.

Hutchins, J., & Somers, H. (1992). An Introduction to Machine Translation. Academic Press Limited.

Krimat, N. (2021). The challenge of quality management in crowdsourced translation: the case of the NGO Translators Without Borders. QScience Connect Journal, 3.

Rico Pérez, C. (2019). Mapping translation technology and the multilingual needs of NGOs along the aid chain. In F. Federici & S. O'Brien (eds.). Translation in Cascading Crises (pp. 112-132). Routledge.

Tesseur, W. (2022). Translation as Social Justice : Translation Policies and Practices in Non-Governmental Organisations. Routledge.

HPLT's First Release of Data and Models

Nikolay Arefyev[♣] **Mikko Aulamo**[★] **Pinzhen Chen**[♡] **Ona de Gibert**[★]
Barry Haddow[♡] **Jindřich Helcl**[♠] **Bhavitvya Malik**[♡] **Gema Ramírez-Sánchez**[◇]
Pavel Stepachev[♡] **Jörg Tiedemann**[★] **Dušan Variš**[♠] **Jaume Zaragoza**[◇]
[♣]University of Oslo [★]University of Helsinki [♡]University of Edinburgh
[♠]Charles University [◇]Prompsit Language Engineering
`https://hplt-project.org`

Abstract

The High Performance Language Technologies (HPLT) project is a 3-year EU-funded project that started in September 2022. It aims to deliver free, sustainable, and reusable *datasets*, *models*, and *workflows* at scale using high-performance computing. We describe the first results of the project. The data release includes monolingual data in 75 languages at 5.6T tokens and parallel data in 18 language pairs at 96M pairs, derived from 1.8 petabytes of web crawls. Building upon automated and transparent pipelines, the first machine translation (MT) models as well as large language models (LLMs) have been trained and released. Multiple data processing tools and pipelines have also been made public.

1 Introduction

The HPLT project combines petabytes of natural language data and large-scale model training. Focusing on different aspects of the project, there are eight partners in the consortium: Charles University in Prague (coordinator), University of Edinburgh, University of Helsinki, University of Oslo, University of Turku, Prompsit Language Engineering, and CESNET and Sigma2 HPC centres.

The project has achieved several milestones in its first half (Sep 2022–Feb 2024). Specifically, 1) we developed essential data tools and training pipelines; 2) we successfully produced the first edition of datasets for 75 languages and 18 language pairs; 3) we trained and released the first batch of LLMs and MT models.

2 First Release

Datasets For the first release, we processed 1.85 petabytes of the Internet Archive and Common-Crawl to create monolingual and parallel corpora. We release them under the permissive `CC0` licence[1] through our project website[2], OPUS[3], and Hugging Face[4]. We also publish through GitHub open-source tools and pipelines to process huge web archive data packages[5] so that our real use case can serve as an example for others inside and outside of the research community. The monolingual data spans 75 languages and contains roughly 5.6 trillion space-separated tokens after deduplication. The bilingual ones focus on low- to medium-resourced languages and cover 18 language pairs, with roughly 1.4 billion tokens computed on the English side and 96 million sentence pairs.

MT Models The main aim of the first HPLT MT model release was to bring together all the tools in the MT model pipeline, to show that they are capable of building a suite of MT models in a mostly automated fashion. The model building also helped us to extrinsically examine the quality of the first HPLT data release—to see if it influences performance when combined with the much larger existing parallel data on Opus. For this reason, we built bilingual models for all the language pairs included in the first HPLT parallel data release.

The release of the MT model weights is through Hugging Face (HF).[6] These are available in both HF and Marian formats, compatible with the `transformers` library and MarianNMT framework.

[1]We do not own any of the text from which these text data have been extracted. We license the actual packaging of these text data under the `CC0` licence ("no rights reserved").
[2]hplt-project.org/datasets/
[3]opus.nlpl.eu/HPLT.php
[4]huggingface.co/datasets/HPLT/hplt_monolingual_v1_2
[5]github.com/hplt-project
[6]huggingface.co/HPLT

Proceedings of the 25th Annual Conference of the European Association for Machine Translation (Volume 2), pages 53–54
June 24-27, 2024 ©2024 European Association for Machine Translation

There is also a repository[7] containing the scripts to download and process the data, and train and evaluate the models. Third-party users can use this repository, together with our tool chain, to completely reproduce our models.

The tooling for the model-building pipeline includes OpusCleaner (for selecting and cleaning training data), OpusTrainer (a data scheduling and data augmenting tool), and OpusPocus (for managing the training process itself). The first two were described in our previous report (Aulamo et al., 2023), whereas OpusPocus is described below.

Pipelines and Tools Besides a significant effort in establishing the data production pipelines, HPLT also develops data analytics, dashboards, and training pipelines.

HPLT Analytics[8] provides a full range of analytics automatically computed on either monolingual or bilingual datasets to help make informed decisions. It shows corpora details, volumes, language, lengths, noise, quality score distributions, and others. Support for language-dependent components has been added for dozens of languages. Automated reports in YAML and PDF are generated from the web application to which a corpus can be uploaded and processed.

OpusPocus[9] is an MT training pipeline manager that abstracts and automates the repetitive parts in training: data preparation, model training, and fine-tuning. A user can run the default training pipelines without knowledge about the implementation details, simply having their training data and an execution command. OpusPocus's main features are: 1) Python implementation given a large user base; 2) modularity: each pipeline step is isolated from others and only requires the outputs from its dependencies; 3) separation of pipeline execution and monitoring; 4) separation of task definition and task execution. In our workflow, OpusCleaner and OpusTrainer could be wrapped in it.

OPUS-MT dashboard[10] (Tiedemann and de Gibert, 2023) is an interface to the OPUS-MT leaderboards that systematically collect benchmark results of publicly available neural MT models. It provides various views on results on a wide range of language pairs for common benchmarks such as WMT test sets, FLORES200, and NTREX. The dashboard makes it possible to compare models of different sizes and different language coverage to facilitate the selection of appropriate solutions for specific applications. Translations of test sets can also be inspected with highlighted string differences to reference translations or the output of alternative models. The tool currently provides performance information for thousands of open MT models including OPUS-MT models and others in the Hugging Face model hub.

OpusDistillery[11] is an end-to-end pipeline for multilingual MT sequence-level distillation to train efficient NMT models. We develop on top of the Firefox Translation Training pipeline (FTT)[12] from the Bergamot project[13]. We have added support for using pre-trained OPUS-MT models, GPU tracking, and multilingual training.

3 Future Plan for Machine Translation

In our next MT model release, we target three aspects. First, we aim to deliver MT models for even lower-resourced languages that HPLT has acquired. Next, we will investigate cost-efficient MT models via distillation, quantization, etc. Finally, in comparison with the current release of unidirectional translation models, we plan to explore massively multilingual models and large language models.

Acknowledgment

This project has received funding from the European Union's Horizon Europe research and innovation programme under Grant agreement No 101070350 and from UK Research and Innovation (UKRI) under the UK government's Horizon Europe funding guarantee [grant number 10052546].

References

Aulamo, Mikko, Nikolay Bogoychev, Shaoxiong Ji, Graeme Nail, Gema Ramírez-Sánchez, Jörg Tiedemann, Jelmer van der Linde, and Jaume Zaragoza. 2023. HPLT: High performance language technologies. In *Proceedings of the 24th Annual Conference of the European Association for Machine Translation.*

Tiedemann, Jörg and Ona de Gibert. 2023. The OPUS-MT dashboard – a toolkit for a systematic evaluation of open machine translation models. In *Proceedings of the 61st Annual Meeting of the Association for Computational Linguistics (Volume 3: System Demonstrations).*

[7] github.com/hplt-project/mt-models
[8] github.com/hplt-project/data-analytics-tool
[9] github.com/hplt-project/OpusPocus
[10] github.com/hplt-project/OPUS-MT-dashboard
[11] github.com/Helsinki-NLP/OpusDistillery
[12] github.com/mozilla/firefox-translations-training
[13] browser.mt

Literacy in Digital Environments and Resources (LT-LiDER)

Pilar Sanchéz Gijón∗, Esther Torres Simon∗, Mireia Vargas Urpí, Nora Aranberri§, Dragoş Ciobanu††, Ana Guerberof Arenas∗∗, Janiça Hackenbuchner‡, Dorothy Kenny†, Ralph Krüger‡, Joss Moorkens†, Miguel Rios Gaona††, Isabel Rivas Ginel†, Caroline Rossi¶, Alina Secară††, Antonio Toral∗∗

∗Universitat Autònoma de Barcelona, †Dublin City University, ‡TH Köln, §University of the Basque Country, ¶Université Grenoble Alpes, ∗∗University of Groningen, ††University of Vienna

Abstract

LT-LiDER is an Erasmus+ cooperation project with two main aims. The first is to map the landscape of technological capabilities required to work as a language and/or translation expert in the digitalised and datafied language industry. The second is to generate training outputs that will help language and translation trainers improve their skills and adopt appropriate pedagogical approaches and strategies for integrating data-driven technology into their language or translation classrooms, with a focus on digital and AI literacy.

1 Introduction

Although translation trainers and professionals are no strangers to integrating tools into their workflows, increasingly complex Natural Language Processing (NLP) technologies based on contemporary AI research are now either incorporated into existing tools or may be used alongside them. These technologies are often based on previous translation or workflow management data and are predictive (and generative), with capabilities of modifying digital language processes and automating portions of translators' tasks.

Where once these technologies were easy to understand and conceptualise, the growing degree of complexity of these technologies and the continuous development of new models in quick succession can make it very difficult for language experts to follow how they can be applied to their work successfully. This increased opacity "is a particular cause for concern for humans required to work with contemporary MT systems because it can limit their ability to intervene in translation workflows, thus undermining agendas of translator empowerment" (Kenny 2019, 438). Furthermore, many commercial systems that reuse copyrighted data market themselves as solutions to further automate translation workflows to increase productivity and save time and money without necessarily providing supporting evidence.

The Literacy in Digital Environments and Resources (LT-LiDER) cooperation partnership consortium, consisting of researchers and lecturers with substantial experience in NLP and translation technologies, intends to improve this information deficit with two main aims. The first is to map the landscape of technological capabilities required to work as a language and/or translation expert in the digitalised and datafied translation industry. The second is to generate training outputs that will help language and translation trainers improve their skills and adopt appropriate pedagogical approaches and strategies for integrating technology into their language or translation classrooms, with a focus on digital and AI literacy. The strategies and content will introduce the many technical and ethical questions about use and reuse of data, appropriate and risky uses of technology, and positive and negative impacts on the many stakeholders in a translation process. The project thus introduces themes from applied ethics for trainers and translators to make ethically-grounded decisions based on previous learning, and to reflect on the effects of these decisions.

2 Previous work

The LT-LiDER project follows on from previous initiatives led by members of the consortium, such as MultiTraiNMT (Kenny 2022), which created, tested, and disseminated open access materials to improve neural machine translation (MT) teaching and learning among students, teachers, and professional translators across Europe, FOIL, offering online translation industry-focused training,[1] the DigiLing project offering e-learning resources for understanding and exploiting language content in a

[1] See https://foil.cti.gr/ and https://www.digiling.eu/

Proceedings of the 25th Annual Conference of the European Association for Machine Translation (Volume 2), pages 55–56
June 24-27, 2024 ©2024 European Association for Machine Translation

digital era, and the DataLit^{MT} project (Hackenbuchner & Krüger 2023), which developed didactic materials for teaching data and MT literacy. The subsequent rapid emergence of generative tools based on large language models (LLMs) highlights the urgent need for materials to help students and trainers understand the role of data and machine learning, as intended within this project that builds on members' knowledge and experience.

3 Project aims and outputs

This project has three main objectives that will result in several concrete outputs:

- To raise awareness among language and translation experts (professionals and trainers) about the importance of understanding current technologies and how to apply them.

- To create training resources to assist language and translation professionals, trainers, and trainees in applying current technologies.

- To disseminate results from the early stages of the project to maximise its visibility, capture professional trainers' and professionals' attention, and incorporate their feedback in the process.

The first objective is to map and raise awareness of the technological skills gap. To achieve this, we will conduct interviews with relevant stakeholders to identify their current use of technologies, specific needs, and requirements for professionals. These interviews will be recorded and published as videos on the project website. They will also be used to map the technologies used and needed in language learning and translation contexts, and to produce an inventory of scenarios that can be applied in training settings, ranging from formal education to continuous professional development. Relatedly, we intend to create a didactic tool for acquiring MT literacy based on the open-source MutNMT tool, which was developed as part of the MultiTraiNMT project.[2]

The second objective is to provide training and materials to enhance digital and AI literacy skills among language and translation professionals and trainers. For this, we will produce a handbook taking a practical approach to adopting and applying the newest technologies in the language industry. We will also organise a training event involving authors and participants from the target groups of the book to ensure the internal coherence of the handbook and the appropriateness of the content and approach for target users. As a complement to the book, we will prepare training activities in video or written format and organise a learning event where these scenarios will be put to the test, asking trainers and trainees to solve similar problems. This feedback will provide the means to evaluate the effectiveness of the material and to adjust to improve their educational value.

Finally, we will design a questionnaire drawing from surveys, interviews, and, most importantly, the book, to enable self-assessment of related competencies and identify personal needs regarding digital and AI literacy to further develop the training scenarios and learning activities.

4 Future-proofing translation training

This project aims to create materials and resources to facilitate trainers, students, and professionals in a dynamic time of technological advances. The intention is to be flexible enough to incorporate changes as they occur and to produce graduates with the literacies to thrive in multilingual workplaces without losing the core linguistic skills that professionals are required to have. By tackling the need for resources to enhance digital literacy in translation and language-related professions, we address two UN Sustainable Development Goals (SDGs). We address SDG4, Quality Education, by improving how we teach digital literacy to ensure that language and translation students will have the skills and knowledge necessary to succeed in a rapidly evolving digital landscape. Digital literacy is increasingly important for job readiness and employability. By improving digital literacy (addressing SDG8 on Decent Work and Economic Growth) individuals can enhance their skills and competitiveness in the job market, leading to improved economic opportunities and growth.

Acknowledgment

This project is funded from 2023-26 by Erasmus+ as a cooperation partnership in higher education, grant number KA220-HED-15E72916.

References

Kenny, Dorothy, 2019. Machine translation. In: Rawling, Piers/Wilson, Philip (Eds.): The Routledge handbook of translation and philosophy. London: Routledge, 428–445.

Kenny, Dorothy. 2022. *Machine translation for everyone: Empowering users in the age of artificial intelligence*. Language Science Press, Berlin, Germany.

Hackenbuchner, Janiça, and Krüger, Ralph. 2023. DataLit^{MT} – Teaching data literacy in the context of machine translation literacy. In *EAMT 2023*. https://aclanthology.org/2023.eamt-1.28

[2] http://multitrainmt.eu

Cultural Transcreation with LLMs as a new product

Beatriz Silva[1], Helena Wu[1 2 3], Yan Jingxuan[1], Vera Cabarrão[1], Helena Moniz[2 3], Sara Guerreiro de Sousa[1], João Almeida[1], Malene Sjørslev Søholm[1], Catarina Farinha[1], Paulo Dimas[1]

[1]Unbabel, Lisbon, Portugal
[2]University of Lisbon, Portugal
[3]INESC-ID, Lisbon, Portugal
{beatriz.silva, helena.wu.int, yan.jingxuan.int, vera.cabarrao, helena, sara.guerreiro, joao.tiago.almeida, malene.soeholm, catarina.farinha, pdimas}@unbabel.com

Abstract

We present how at Unbabel we have been using large language models (LLMs) to apply a cultural transcreation product on customer support emails and how we have been testing the quality and potential of this product. We discuss our preliminary evaluation of the performance of different MT models in the task of translating rephrased content and the quality of the translation outputs. Furthermore, we introduce the live pilot programme and the corresponding relevant findings, showing that transcreated content is not only culturally adequate but it is also of high rephrasing and translation quality.

1 Introduction

As defined by Díaz-Millón and Olvera-Lobo (2021:358), transcreation is "a type of translation characterized by the intra-interlingual adaptation or re-interpretation of a message intended to suit a target audience (...) paying special attention to the cultural characteristics of the target audience". While transcreation has multiple uses and areas to which it can be applied to, our focus is on the cultural dimension, particularly in the field of machine translation in the domain of customer support, exploring in a near future the extrapolation to other domains, such as marketing. Our goal is to enable companies to move to markets distant from their culture while feeling confident that they will be able to effectively communicate with their customers.

Our approach involves prompting an LLM for rephrasing the source text produced by the customer support (CS) agents in English, before the text is translated with an MT model into the target languages (TL) of Japanese (JA), Korean (KO) and Mandarin Chinese (ZH). Our product can adapt messages in the source to the culture of the target audience without depending on the knowledge of the agent, making the final message culturally appropriate and, thus, improving communication between both parties, as shown in **Figure 1**.

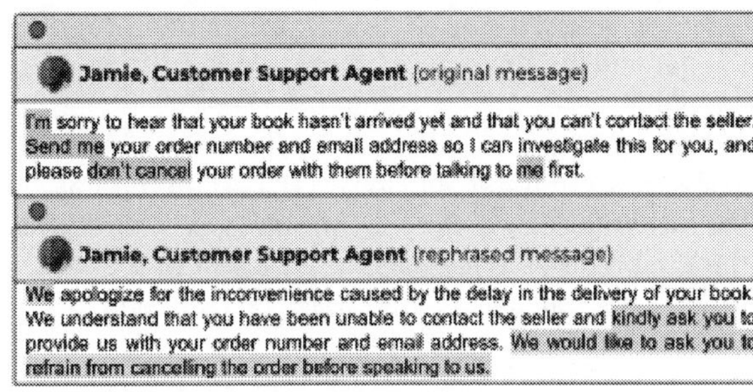

Figure 1: Rephrasing example for JA as TL

2 Prompts and MT Quality

The first step in our transcreation task was to construct the rephrasing prompts for each of the TL. This was achieved through compiling the findings of our research on cultural and linguistic aspects of the TG, specifically regarding CS communication etiquette, as well as the input of native speakers, who are linguistic experts, and non-native speakers, which have lived in these countries for a period of time and learned the language there, into language specific guidelines. As languages which live in the confucianist cultural sphere of influence, our object languages share characteristics such as conveying politeness by showing deference and honoring the interlocutor (Kádár and Mills, 2011). However, the degree and form through which these should be applied differ between them and, thus, different prompts were built depending on the TL.

The next step was ensuring that the content rephrased in the source using our prompts could produce high-quality translations. In order to test this, we translated a total of approximately 1000 rephrased segments distributed across three language pairs (LPs): ~400 segments for EN–JA and EN–KO

Proceedings of the 25th Annual Conference of the European Association for Machine Translation (Volume 2), pages 56–57
June 24-27, 2024 ©2024 European Association for Machine Translation

and ~200 for EN–ZH, with six different MT providers (Azure, AWS, DeepL, Google, ChatGPT and GPT-4) and annotated the outputs so the quality of the translations could be evaluated through Multidimensional Quality Metrics (MQM) framework scores (Lommel *et al.* 2014). The resulting average scores were of around 88 MQM for both en–ja and en–ko, with en–zh scoring higher with an average of 94.3 MQM, reflecting that different MT engines can be successful in the task of translating rephrased content with no adaptation or customization. In addition, by running an automatic quality estimation metric (QE) (Kepler *et al.* 2019) on the translation of the original message and their rephrased versions for the three LPs, we could see that the transcreated messages score higher on average, thus indicating that cultural transcreation (CT) has the potential to improve translation quality.

For the purpose of testing our CT product, we have integrated it into a CS platform in the form of a widget with a "Rephrase" button which calls an API endpoint attached to the CT service after a pre-processing step, including data anonymization. The service relies on an LLM (GPT-4), to rephrase the message according to the prompts, and returns the final rephrased message to the agent in seconds, ready to be translated and sent to the recipient.

3 Live Pilot Programme

Three customers were selected for our pilot evaluation and the data produced during this period, namely the original text, the rephrased text, and the target text (MT version sent to recipients), are being continuously assessed and analyzed quality-wise.

During the first three weeks of the pilot, around three hundred CS emails (based on traffic volume per language) were rephrased: 58.7% for JA, 30.3% for ZH and 11% for KO. In terms of CT quality, almost all the rephrased texts achieved the target-culturalization, and only about 8% were not culturally aware, but no critical level of errors were found. The more frequent rephrasing failures in all three languages were unnatural expressions, inappropriate word substitutions, and errors in the format of greetings and closings.

3.1 LLM Comparison

In order to optimize the prompt version and to choose whether the product needs to update the LLM used and which LLM to adopt specifically, we have been observing and recording the bugs and feedback based on the progress of the pilot evaluation. One month into the pilot, a third version of the prompts for each of the three languages was built on top of the second version. Then, three LLMs were chosen for comparison: GPT-3.5-turbo-16k-0613, GPT-4 and GPT-4-turbo-preview. In this phase the rephrasing outputs were assessed manually in order to evaluate their performance, namely cultural adequateness and adopted prompt rules, and select the most suitable LLM for this task. The final comparison showed that the best performing model was GPT-3.5-turbo-16k-0613 for JA, GPT-4 for KO, and GPT-4-turbo-preview for ZH.

With the continuous quality monitoring, the improvement of the prompts and the LLM comparison, many of the issues have been reduced. For example, the greetings and closings format errors in EN–ZH rephrasing no longer occur in the latest pilot data. These changes may not only be influenced by the optimization factors of prompts, but also due to the improved compliance and stability of the latest versions of the LLM.

3.2 Future Work

As ongoing work, we are including this product in the translation pipeline for other customers, languages and domains. This is supported in the high quality of the rephrasing, its impact on the MT quality without any customization or adaptation, and the flexibility of managing the best LLM per language with automatic metrics (e.g. QE).

Acknowledgements

This work was developed within the scope of the project n° 62 - "Center for Responsible AI", financed by European Funds, namely "Recovery and Resilience Plan - Component 5: Agendas Mobilizadoras para a Inovação Empresarial", included in the NextGenerationEU funding program and was partially founded by FCT, Fundação para a Ciência e a Tecnologia, under project UIDB /50021/2020(DOI:10.54499/UIDB/50021/2020).

References

Díaz-Millón, M., & Olvera-Lobo, M.D. (2021). Towards a definition of transcreation: A systematic literature review. *Perspectives, 31(2),* 347–364

Kádár, D., & Mills, S. (2011). Politeness in east Asia: An introduction. *Cambridge University Press,* 1–17

Lommel, A., Burchardt, A., Popović, M., Harris, K., Avramidis, E. & Uszkoreit, H. (2014). Using a new analytic measure for the annotation and analysis of MT errors on real data. Mauro Cettolo *et al.* (eds) (2014) *Proceedings of the 17th Annual Conference of the European Association for Machine Translation.* Dubrovnik: European Association for Machine Translation, 165–172

Kepler, F., Trénous, J., Terviso, M., Vera, M. & Martins, André F. T. (2019). OpenKiwi: An Open Source Framework for Quality Estimation. arXiv:1902.08646

AI4Culture: Towards Multilingual Access for Cultural Heritage Data

Tom Vanallemeersch, Sara Szoc, Laurens Meeus
CrossLang NV, Franklin Rooseveltlaan 348/8, 9000 Gent, Belgium
{firstname.lastname}@crosslang.com

Abstract

The AI4Culture project (2023–2025), funded by the European Commission, and involving a 12-partner consortium led by the National Technical University of Athens, develops a platform serving as an online capacity building hub for AI technologies in the cultural heritage (CH) sector, enabling multilingual access to CH data. It offers access to AI-related resources, including openly labelled datasets for model training and testing, deployable and reusable tools, and capacity building materials. The tools are aimed at optical character recognition (OCR) for printed and handwritten documents, subtitle generation and validation, machine translation (MT), and metadata enrichment via image information extraction and semantic linking. The project also customises these tools to enhance interface and component usability. We illustrate this with technology that corrects OCR output using language models and adapts it for MT.

1 Introduction

The AI4Culture project aims to develop an online capacity building hub for AI technologies in the cultural heritage (CH) sector. This innovative platform seeks to make CH data more accessible and understandable in today's multilingual digital era, by facilitating data sharing, promoting cultural content reuse and linking the vast European data space (which ensures data availability for economic, societal and research use) with CH institutions.

The project is funded by the European Commission (EC) and runs from April 2023 to March 2025. The consortium is led by the AILS Laboratory of the National Technical University of Athens (NTUA). The other consortium partners are the NTUA spin-off Datoptron and organisations specialised in digital CH (i.e. Europeana Foundation, European Fashion Heritage Association, the DigitGLAM unit at University of Leuven, and the company Datable), natural language processing (the companies CrossLang and Pangeanic, the MT Research Unit at Fondazione Bruno Kessler (FBK), the Digital Safety and Security Center of the Austrian Institute of Technology), online translation services (the company Translated), and media culture (Institute for Sound and Vision).

The AI4Culture platform, expected to launch its first version mid-2024, will offer access to AI-related resources, i.e. to openly labelled datasets for training and testing models, to deployable and reusable tools, and to capacity building materials on the use of these tools and datasets for training, testing, and evaluation. The platform targets CH students and professionals, data providers, researchers and AI model developers, amongst others. Towards the end of 2024, several workshops will be organised on the technologies involved.

2 Technology and language coverage

The tools made accessible through the platform relate to four technologies:

1. Multilingual text recognition in scanned printed and handwritten documents through optical character recognition (OCR), machine

Proceedings of the 25th Annual Conference of the European Association for Machine Translation (Volume 2), pages 59–60
June 24-27, 2024 ©2024 European Association for Machine Translation

translation (MT), and semi-automatic validation of transcriptions.

2. Automated generation of multilingual subtitles and semi-automatic subtitle validation.

3. Enrichment of CH metadata through information extraction from images (color detection, object detection) and semantic linking (e.g. named entities).

4. Generation of multilingual versions of CH metadata using MT.

Accessibility of the above technologies will be achieved through online interfaces, application programming interfaces (APIs), which allow to send requests to various services, and docker images, which can be locally deployed. The interfaces include Transcribathon[1] (supporting the transcription of documents and the translation of transcriptions), Subbit![2] (supporting the editing of automatically generated subtitles), the interface of SAGE[3] (serving semantic annotation and generation of enrichments), and PECAT[4] (supporting validation and post-editing of automatic translations).

The software built during the project to achieve accessibility will be provided as open source. Moreover, this software focuses on the reuse of existing open-source tools, such as PERO-OCR.[5]

On the multilingual level, the transcription and subtitling services, as well the CH metadata, cover numerous languages, with a focus on EU official languages. The translation functionality uses various systems, including the Europeana Translate[6] and the EC's eTranslation engines.

3 Customisation of technologies

The tools made accessible on the platform are customised to increase the usability of interfaces and components. For instance, FBK's subtitling components incorporate the Whisper[7] pre-trained model for improving speech recognition. Another example is the post-correction component developed by Crosslang, which aims at enhancing both OCR and MT outputs of auto-generated transcriptions. This component particularly targets documents for which no (closely) matching specialised transcription engine exists in terms of language, time period, script of writing, etc.

The OCR post-correction component consist of several steps. First, it removes word-splitting hyphens at line breaks using a language model-based technique. Next, it segments the transcribed lines into sentences using an advanced rule-based approach. Finally, it performs word post-correction through either a basic method using lexicon and language model lookup, or through a computationally more demanding strategy that prompts a chatbot based on a large language model (LLM) to make corrections to the transcriptions.

Figure 1 shows a part of a Dutch letter from World War II.[8] Table 1 compares different OCR[9] and MT outputs[10] for a sentence from this letter, highlighting the effects of the post-correction component on OCR and MT results. The segmentation step leads to an enhancement of the MT output, consisting of a better handling of the non-existent Dutch word *errolinks* (ground truth *er zo links*). The word post-correction step (using the LLM-based method mentioned above) brings the Dutch word closer to its ground truth by replacing it with *er links*, thus further improving the MT output of the sentence (containing *theft* instead of *stolen*).

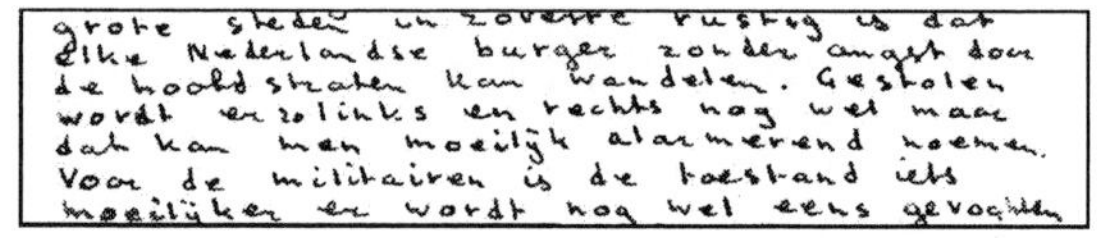
grote steden in zoverre rustig is dat
elke Nederlandse burger zonder angst door
de hoofdstraten kan wandelen. Gestolen
wordt er zo links en rechts nog wel maar
dat kan men moeilijk alarmerend noemen.
Voor de militairen is de toestand iets
moeilijker en wordt nog wel eens gevochten

Figure 1: Part of Dutch letter from World War II

OCR	de hoofdstraten kan wandelen. Gestolen wordt ***errolinks*** en rechts nog
MT	can walk the main streets. ***Stolen it will be erroleft*** and right
Segmented	Gestolen wordt ***errolinks*** en rechts nog
MT	***Stolen*** is still happening on the left and right
Corrected	Gestolen wordt **er links** en rechts nog
MT	There is still **theft** left and right

Table 1: Effect of segmentation and word correction on OCR and MT output

Acknowledgements: AI4Culture is funded by EC's DIGITAL programme (project 101100683).

[1] transcribathon.eu
[2] subbit.eu
[3] pro.europeana.eu/page/sage
[4] pangeanic.com/datasets-for-ai/ai-data-annotation-platform
[5] github.com/DCGM/pero-ocr
[6] pro.europeana.eu/project/europeana-translate
[7] github.com/openai/whisper
[8] zenodo.org/records/8108347 (we converted the background color to white for better contrast in the figure)
[9] Produced by the Text Titan I model from Transkribus (readcoop.eu/transkribus).
[10] Produced by Google Translate.

The Center for Responsible AI Project

Maria Ana Henriques
Unbabel
maria.henriques@unbabel.com

Catarina Farinha
Unbabel
catarina.farinha@unbabel.com

Nuno André, António Novais, Sara Guerreiro de Sousa, Bruno Prezado Silva, Ana Oliveira, Helena Moniz, André Martins, Paulo Dimas
Unbabel
{nuno.andre, antonio.novais, sara.guerreiro, bruno, ana.oliveira, helena, andre.martins, pdimas}@unbabel.com

Abstract

This paper describes the project "NextGenAI: Center for Responsible AI", a 39-month Mobilizing and Green Agenda for Business Innovation funded by the Portuguese Recovery and Resilience Plan, under the Recovery and Resilience Facility (RRF). The project aims to create a new Center for Responsible AI in Portugal, capable of delivering more than 20 AI products in crucial areas like "Life Sciences", many of which use generative AI, particularly NLP models such as those for Machine Translation, contributing to translating into legislation the European Law included in the EU AI Act, and creating a critical mass in the development of responsible AI technologies. To accomplish this mission, the Center for Responsible AI[1] is formed by an ecosystem of start-ups and research institutions driving research in a virtuous way by addressing real market needs and opportunities in Responsible AI.

1 Introduction

McKinsey estimates that Generative AI could add the equivalent of $2.6 trillion to $4.4 trillion annually in value to the global economy — by comparison, more than 10x the Portuguese GDP. This would increase the impact of all artificial intelligence by 15 to 40 percent (Chui et al., 2023). The Center for Responsible AI aims to create the next generation of AI products, delivering business impact in this global market.

However, AI has inherent risks that are limiting its full potential, particularly in critical fields such as Life Sciences, where AI's wrong decisions could endanger lives. Moreover, AI can cause harm to humanity, notably by jeopardizing privacy, exacerbating carbon emissions due to its demanding computational needs, and operating opaquely, impeding understanding of its operations, decision-making processes, and ethical alignment. Responsible AI technologies and principles are the key to bringing all the benefits of AI to humanity while ensuring sustainability and preventing harm.

To accomplish this mission, the Center for Responsible AI is formed by an ecosystem of AI start-ups that will create synergies with top research centers, driving research in a virtuous way by addressing real market needs.. To ensure real-world impact, the consortium includes leading companies in key markets as technology adopters. The Center aims to create or leverage over 20 Responsible AI products[2], many of which use generative AI, particularly NLP models such as those for Machine Translation while creating a critical mass of knowledge and talent in Responsible AI technologies. This initiative seeks to establish Europe as a global leader in Responsible AI, influencing principles and regulations in this domain, and contributing to EU AI legislation.

2 Project overview

The Center for Responsible AI's proposal received approval for a total investment of around €78 million that will be executed from October 2021 to December 2025. The Center's overall mission is to revolutionize the AI landscape responsibly and to develop the next generation of AI products that are explainable, fair, trustworthy, and sustainable. The project's main goals can be summarized as follows:

- Create the next generation of AI products driven by Responsible AI technologies by promoting a

[1] https://centerforresponsible.ai/

[2] https://centerforresponsible.ai/products/

Proceedings of the 25th Annual Conference of the European Association for Machine Translation (Volume 2), pages 60–61
June 24-27, 2024 ©2024 European Association for Machine Translation

virtuous cycle between start-ups, research centers, and industry leaders. These products will have a real impact on society and solve new use cases for AI, opening new business opportunities in sensitive domains like Life Sciences, but also in crucial sectors like Retail and Tourism.

- Spearhead R&D efforts focused on practical solutions for universal challenges. From R&D teams at leading tech start-ups to world-class academic researchers, the Center focuses on applying cutting-edge research to everyday problems, tackling tangible issues using a responsible AI framework.

- Address crucial AI use cases through advanced machine learning and natural language processing approaches, including Machine Translation.

- Position Europe as a world leader in principles and policies of Responsible AI to influence European regulation which will be key to the future development of AI products.

- Retain and attract the best AI talent worldwide, the key ingredient to invent the future. This talent circulates from academia to start-ups transferring the knowledge that drives innovation into products.

2.1 Key partners and people

The Center is made up of ten start-ups (Unbabel, Automaise, Emotai, NeuralShift, Priberam, Visor.ai, YData, Youverse, and two unicorns - Feedzai and Sword Health), eight research centers (Champalimaud Foundation, CISUC, FEUP, Fraunhofer Portugal AICOS, INESC-ID, IST, IST-ID/ISR and IT), a law firm (Vieira de Almeida) and five industry leaders in Life Sciences, Tourism and Retail (BIAL, Centro Hospitalar de São João, Luz Saúde, Grupo Pestana and SONAE).

2.2 Methodology

New mechanisms were put in place to facilitate the contacts between research centers and start-ups which significantly contribute to shortening the time required to transfer technologies from low TRLs[3] to a commercialization stage. To this end, the project was organized in 2 main streams:

1. The "Product Pods", *i.e.*, smaller groups within the Consortium that put together research centers, start-ups, and technology takers centered on developing a specific product/technology, promoting the creation of a virtuous Research & Innovation circle. The Consortium architecture promotes this virtuous circle as it was designed for start-ups to bring product-driven research challenges to research centers. In this way, the Center's top AI research groups will be inspired to solve hard problems that will create market value, giving these products a competitive advantage globally.

2. Research Projects, in which the Center's highly qualified research teams tackle complex research challenges that may not have a direct market application yet. However, the ultimate goal of the project is to promote an ecosystem in which the fundamental research being pursued lead to future product innovation in AI companies. The ongoing research projects can be grouped into 5 main areas: (i) Energy-Efficient and Sustainable AI; (ii) Privacy-Preserving AI Systems; (iii) Transparent, Fair, and Explainable AI; (iv) Language Technologies and Embodied Human-AI Interaction; and (v) Multilingual and Contextualized Conversational AI.

2.3 Current outcomes

The project has already accomplished the following outcomes:

- 18 product pods were created to develop AI products powered by Responsible AI technologies. An example is Unbabel's "Translation for High Risk Content" which aims to offer a responsible way to produce AI-enabled translations in domains in which critical translation errors cannot be tolerated;
- 163 highly qualified jobs have been created;
- 40 PhDs and MScs are currently in progress;
- More than 20 scientific papers were published (e.g. Guerreiro et al., 2024 - which recently got accepted to TACL);
- 10 patent applications have been submitted or are under submission;
- €19 million has been invested in AI;
- A Position Letter[4] with recommendations for the EU AI Act was released.

3 Acknowledgements

This work was supported by the Portuguese Recovery and Resilience Plan (PRR) through project C645008882-00000055, Center for Responsible AI.

References

Chui, M., Hazan, E., Roberts, R., Singla, A., Smaje, K., Sukharevsky, A., Yee, L., & Zemmel, R. (2023, June 14). The economic potential of generative AI: The next productivity frontier. McKinsey & Company.

Guerreiro, N. M., Rei, R., van Stigt, D., Coheur, L., Colombo, P., & Martins, A. F. (2023). xcomet: Transparent machine translation evaluation through fine-grained error detection. arXiv preprint arXiv:2310.10482.

[3] Technology Readiness Level

[4] https://centerforresponsible.ai/eu-ai-act-position-letter/

The EAMT organisers gratefully acknowledge the support from the following sponsors.

Silver

Bronze

Collaborators

Supporters

SPRINGER NATURE

Media Sponsors

MultiLingual

Author Index

Association for Computational Linguistics
209 N. Eighth Street
Stroudsburg, Pennsylvania 18360

CURRAN ASSOCIATES INC.
proceedings.com

ISBN 979-8-3313-0477-5
9 798331 304775

First Workshop on Trustworthy Natural Language Processing (TrustNLP 2021)

Online
10 June 2021